Linda Eder
It's Time

Photography by *Davis Factor*
Piano/Vocal Arrangements by *Edwin McLean*

It's Time is available from Atlantic Records (82977-2)

For a comprehensive listing of Cherry Lane Music's songbooks, sheet music,
instructional materials, videos and more, check out our entire catalog on the
Internet. Our home page address is: http://www.cherrylane.com

Que

I have to say that I feel completely blessed to be in the position that I now find myself. I have recorded an album of songs that I am proud to sing, songs which deserve the long lives that I believe they will have thanks to Atlantic Records and Cherry Lane Music. The process of creating this album was long, involved, and wonderful!

There are so many reasons to love Frank Wildhorn that he really doesn't need to write music. The fact that he writes so amazingly well makes me one of the luckiest women and singers in the world. When I told Frank that I wanted to record this style of music, he dove right in without batting an eye. Suddenly the ghosts of Gershwin, Porter, Berlin, and Kern were alive in our piano. Their influence was everywhere. But what came out of that piano was pure Wildhorn–lovely, haunting, joyous melodies. All they needed were the right lyrics.

Singing has always been very personal to me, which is why lyrics are important and become more so every year. And for this reason, I thank the stars that led Jack Murphy to our door. In Jack, Frank found the perfect writing partner and I found someone willing to listen to some of my crazy ideas and turn them into lyrics. The result of this teaming was magical. They have created a repertoire of material that is intelligent, witty, heartbreaking and so rare in this modern, angry world.

Because I have lived with many of the songs on the album, performing them in concerts across the country, they have become musically and emotionally comfortable. This familiarity is what made the recording process that much more fun. We assembled an incredible group of

rture

Linda with composer Frank Wildhorn and lyricist Jack Murphy.

musicians to record the new big band arrangements and I could have listened to them play all night. It was a thrill to sing with them and to share the excitement. Each new chart came to glorious life in that New York studio. There is nothing quite like it!

So many people worked long hours to make this album happen. I personally have never worked so hard on anything in my life. Because I was producing with Frank, I had to be there even when it was three o'clock in the morning and my ears were fried from listening to a track for the two hundredth time. The quality of the songwriting got me through. I never get tired of the melodies or lyrics. I have to believe that many people will share my feelings. This type of songwriting craft has become very rare in these days of fragmented charts. It is seldom attempted and as a result singers looking for this type of material are forced to return to the old standards. So it is with great pleasure that we bring you an album of 'new standards'—songs as beautifully crafted as the songs of old, new yet wonderfully familiar to the romantic in all of us.

I am honored to be the person to introduce them to you. I know you will find as much joy in them as I have. "It's Time" for new standards.

Take care,

Linda Eder

Linda Eder

"In Jack, Frank found the perfect writing partner. The result of this teaming was magical. They have created a repertoire of material that is intelligent, witty, heartbreaking and so rare in this modern, angry world."

– Linda

It's Time

Intermission with Linda follows page 45

The Players

Frank Wildhorn

From the first time Linda and I felt the thrill of hearing our big band roar to one of Kim Scharnberg's great new charts, to Linda and Jeremy Robert's two o'clock in the morning "one take" performance recording of "Over The Rainbow," the making of *It's Time* has left me with some of the best memories in my life of making music.

It is a beautiful thing when so many elements of a project come together as they have on these sessions. Jack Murphy's lyrics, written exclusively for Linda, are a combination of grace, wit, craft, and romance, and no one brings life to a good lyric like Linda. Jeremy Roberts, Ed Maina, Dave Finck, Mark Walker, and all the musicians played with great style and passion, which you can hear on every track.

This project was a great challenge for us as we tried to take the listener on a journey from the worlds of big band, swing, and jazz influenced material, through the colors and rhythms of theater and pop. With Linda—whose glorious voice continues to astound me every day—as our guide, this project has been a most extraordinary musical journey, and all I can say is I can't wait to start our next one!

Enjoy,

Composer of Jekyll & Hyde: The Musical, *and many songs in this collection.*

Jack Murphy

In a perfect world, a lyricist hears his or her lyrics sung by a perfect singer—one who not only hits the notes, but reads the lyric with a subtlety and nuance the lyricist could only imagine. In a perfect world, the lyricist can devote his or her energies to writing the lyric, secure in the knowledge that the singer will give a depth to the words that can't possibly exist on the printed page. In a perfect world, the lyricist hears his or her words sung by the perfect singer, who always makes him sound smarter and better than he really is. For this lyricist, Linda Eder has created the perfect world.

Lyricist of many songs in this collection.

Leslie Bricusse

LINDA, lovely Linda Eder!–
I know no-one who sings better!
No-one since I heard the ice-and-
Diamond fire of Barbra Streisand.
And, among its thousand thrills,

EDER's voice excites and chills–
Dazzles us with every bar!
Eder is what so few are–
Ready made a superstar!

*Lyricist of "Someone Like You" and "A New Life"
from* Jekyll & Hyde: The Musical.

Ahmet M. Ertegün

In my many years in music, I've had the opportunity to hear several aspiring young singers. Once in a while, I hear some-one with a special voice that has the power of communication. Linda Eder possesses such a voice, and a style that is both theatrical and personal. She is joined here by composer and producer Frank Wildhorn, whose music she infuses with meaning and feeling.

I hope that Linda's voice—from its most delicate to its most dramatic—will move you as much as it has moved me.

Chairman/CEO Atlantic Records

Maury Yeston

Linda Eder has a natural vocal gift, rarely found, with an extraordinary beauty and range that casts an instantaneous spell on all who hear her.

Composer and lyricist of "Unusual Way" from the musical Nine.

It's Time

Words by Jack Murphy
Music by Frank Wildhorn

Moderately slow

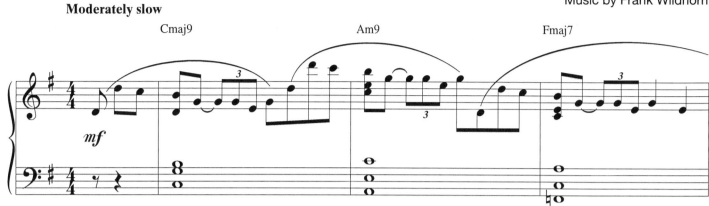

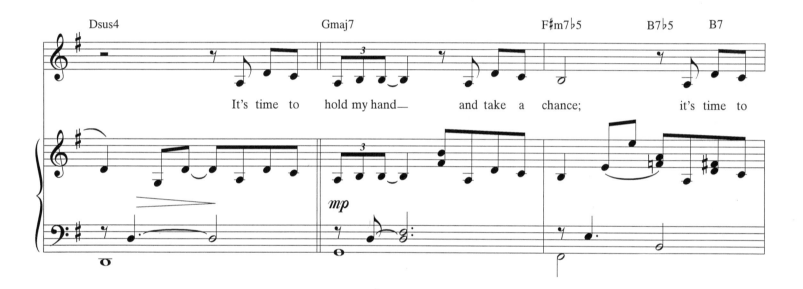

It's time to hold my hand— and take a chance; it's time to

pay the band— and start the dance. We hear the mel-o-dy,— we know the

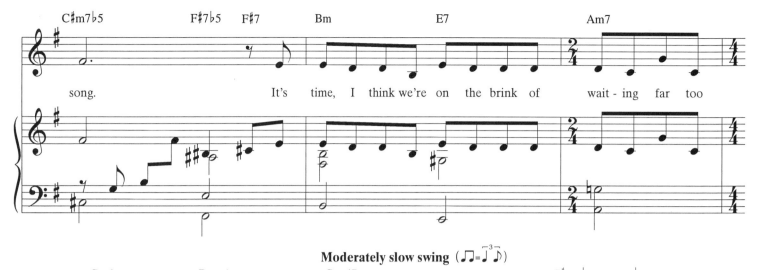

song.   It's time, I think we're on the brink of wait - ing far too

Moderately slow swing (♫ = ♩³♪)

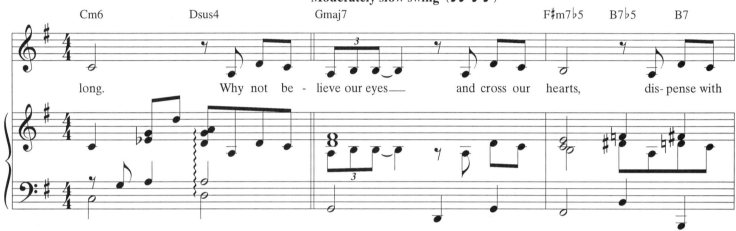

long. Why not be - lieve our eyes____ and cross our hearts, dis - pense with

al - i - bis,____ e - nough false starts. It's time to put a - way____ our child - ish

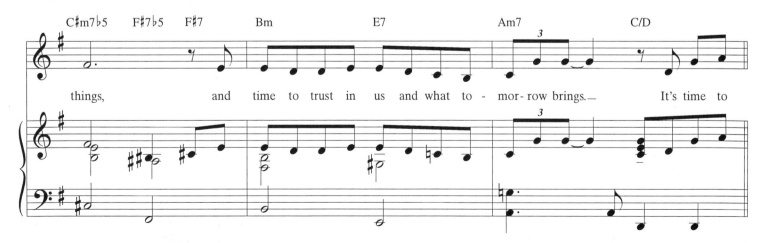

things, and time to trust in us and what to - mor - row brings.____ It's time to

risk it all—— and shoot the moon; so just let go and fall,—— it's not too

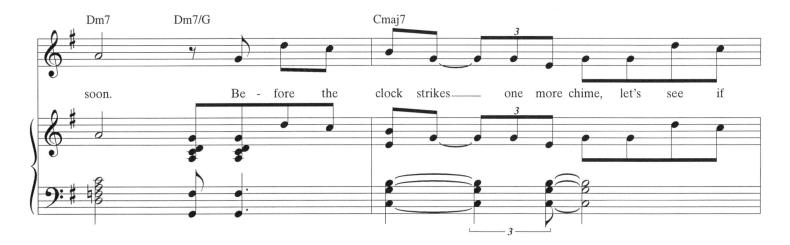

soon. Be - fore the clock strikes—— one more chime, let's see if

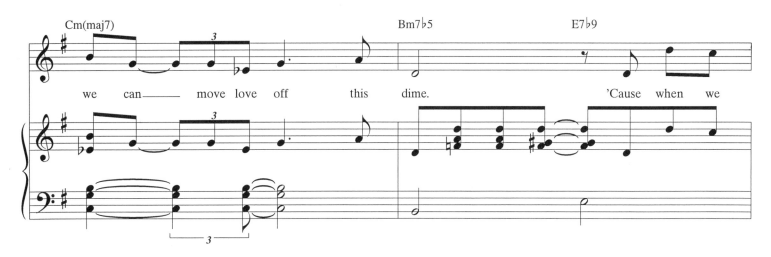

we can—— move love off this dime. 'Cause when we

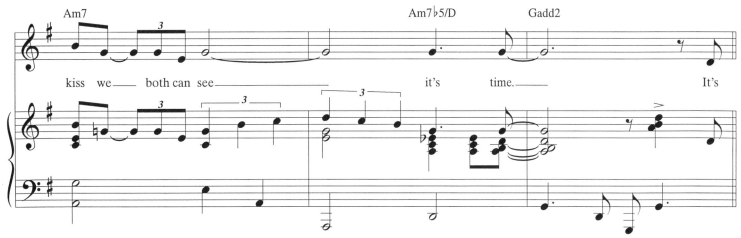

kiss we—— both can see—— it's time.—— It's

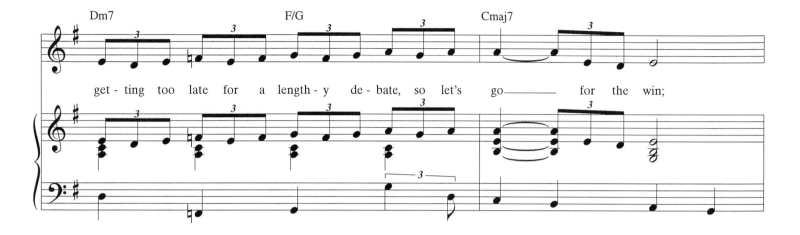

get - ting too late for a length - y de - bate, so let's go———— for the win;

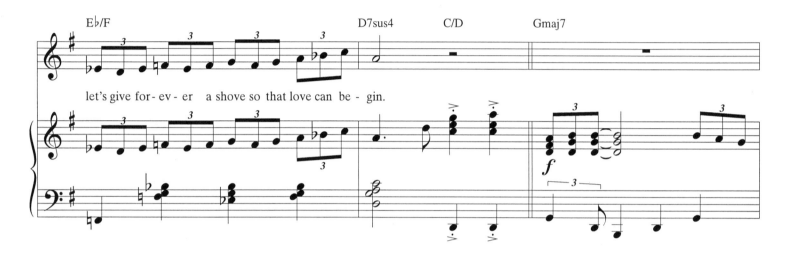

let's give for - ev - er a shove so that love can be - gin.

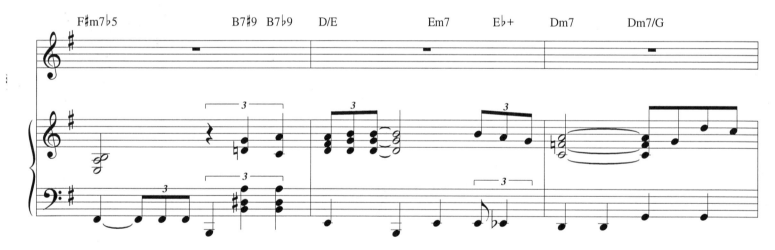

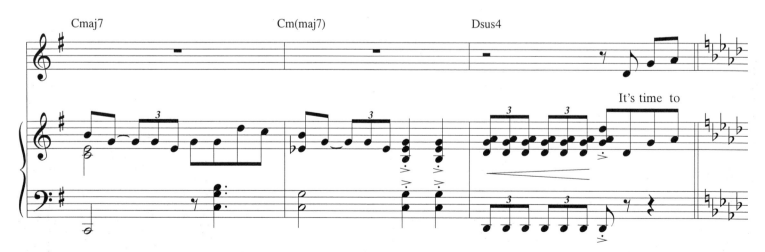

It's time to

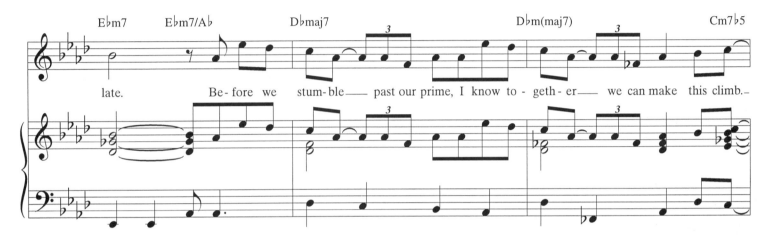

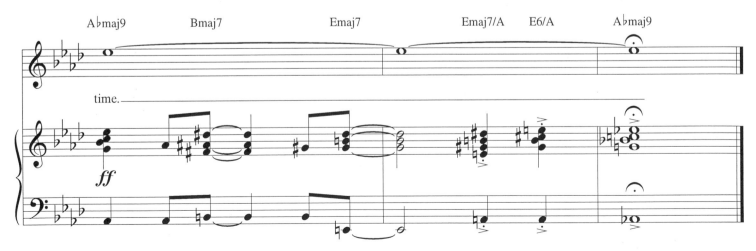

I Want More

Words by Jack Murphy
Music by Frank Wildhorn

Moderately fast

Day in and out, what my life's all a-bout are the things that you find far too
I need at-ten-tion, not mere con-de-scen-sion, but you just don't get the dis-
When did the "me" that I so long to be lose her nat-u-ral sense of di-

bor-ing.
tinc-tion.
rec-tion?

Wash-ing and cook-ing and
Push-ing and shov-ing does
When did the you that I'm

all,   af - ter all?   I   want
last,   will it last?   I   want

mag - ic car - pets, I want true ro-mance.—— I want moon - light cruis - es to the
Shake-speare son - nets, I want oohs and ahs.—— I want long - stem ros - es in a

south of France. And I want kiss - es that go on for days;—— I want
Guc - ci vase. And I want kiss - es that go on for days:—— I want

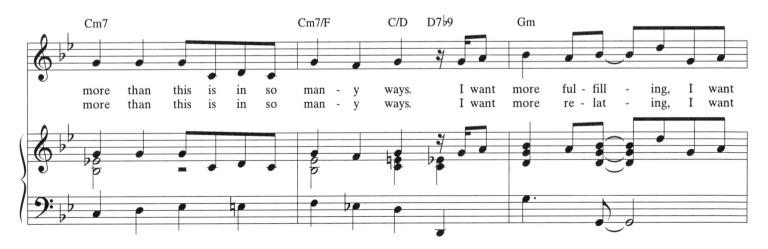

more than this is in so man - y ways. I want more ful - fill - ing, I want
more than this is in so man - y ways. I want more re - lat - ing, I want

14

e - qual bill - ing. I want cham-pagne chill - ing at the door. So in
less de - bat - ing. I want all those things__ I'm wait - ing for. So in

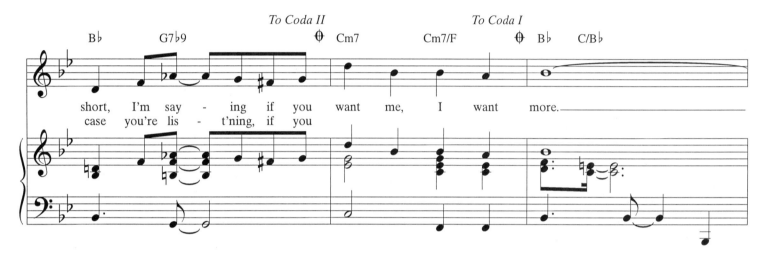

short, I'm say - ing if you want me, I want more.__
case you're lis - t'ning, if you

D.S. (take 2nd ending) al Coda I

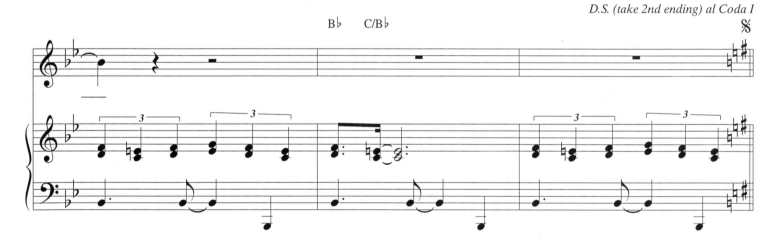

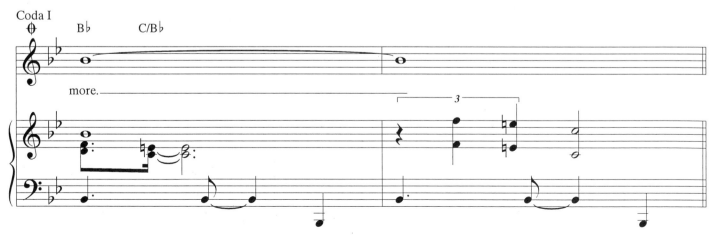

Coda I

more.__

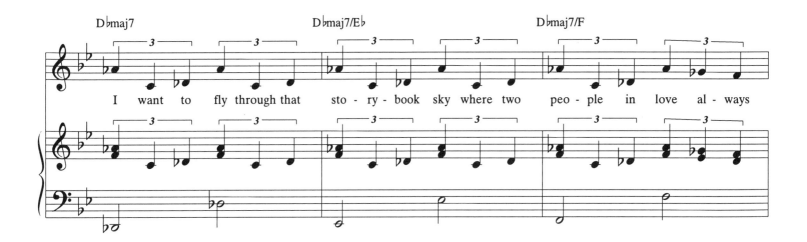

I want to fly through that sto - ry - book sky where two peo - ple in love al - ways

trav - el. I want to be like some deep mys - ter - y that you

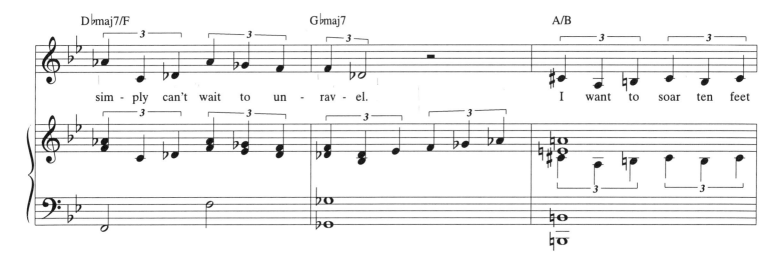

sim - ply can't wait to un - rav - el. I want to soar ten feet

D.S. (a tempo; lyric 1) al Coda II

off of the floor when you walk through the door like I used to be - fore.___ I want

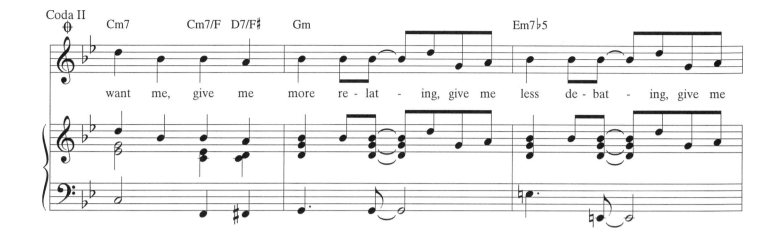

want me, give me more re-lat-ing, give me less de-bat-ing, give me

all those things— I'm wait-ing for. So in case you're lis-t'ning, if you want me, real-ly

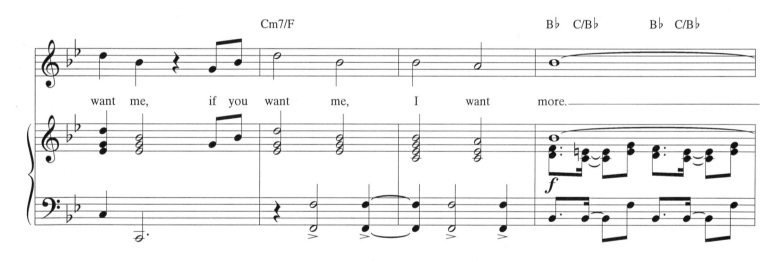

want me, if you want me, I want more.————

I'm Afraid This Must Be Love

Words by Jack Murphy
Music by Frank Wildhorn

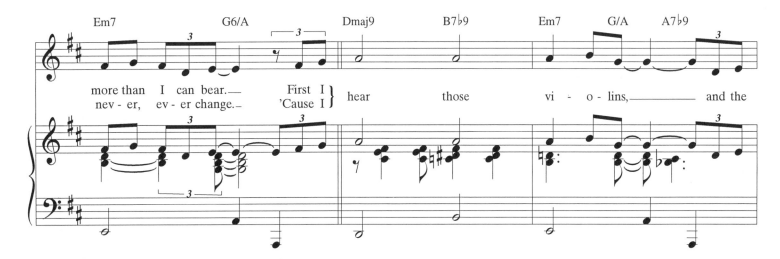

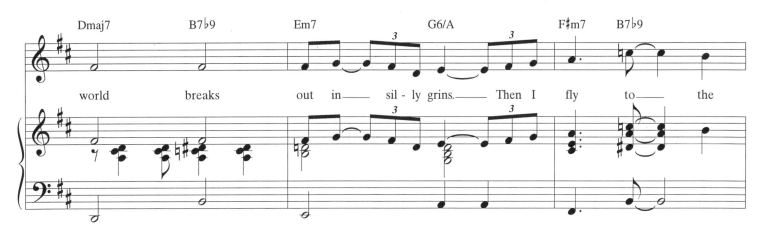

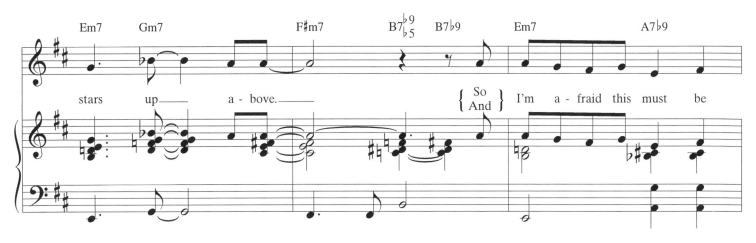

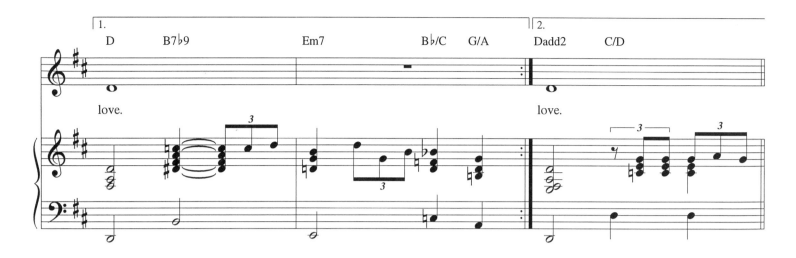

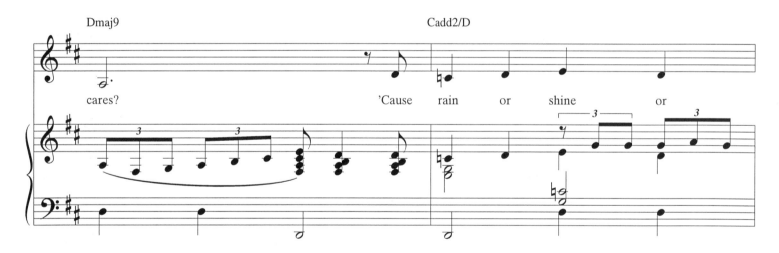

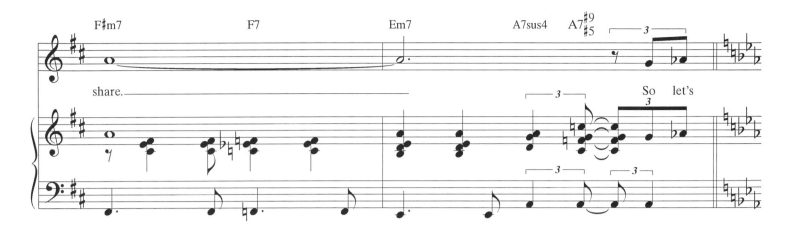

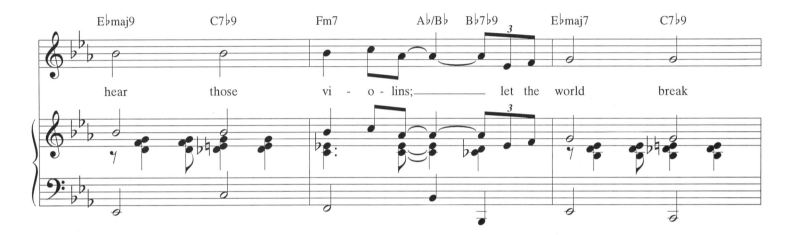

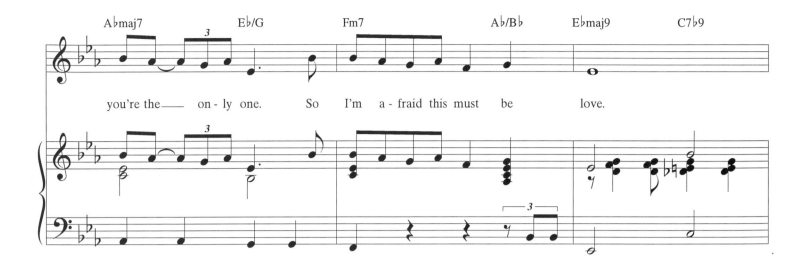

you're the— on - ly one.   So   I'm a - fraid this must   be   love.

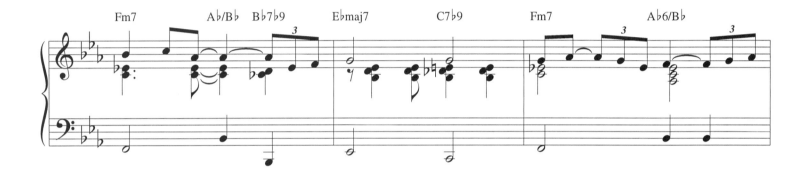

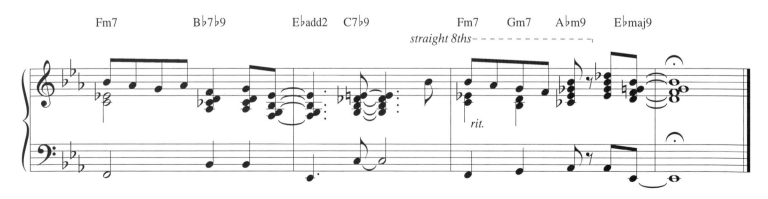

Don't Ask Me Why

Words by Jack Murphy
Music by Frank Wildhorn and Linda Eder

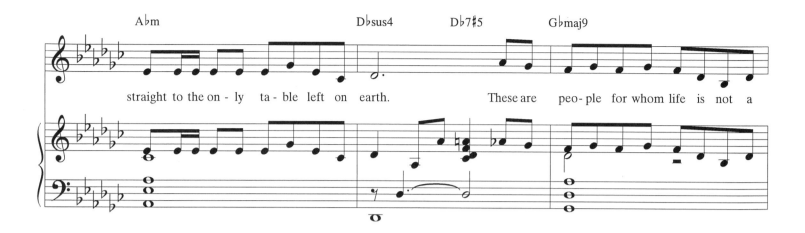

straight to the on - ly ta - ble left on earth.   These are   peo - ple for whom life is not a

chal - lenge;____ they've got   sa - voir-faire that ooz - es ped - i - gree.   They're the

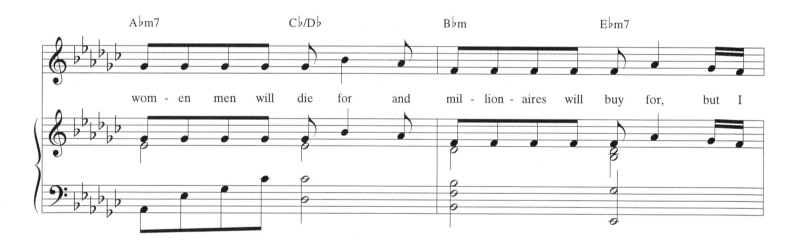

wom - en men will   die   for   and   mil - lion - aires will   buy   for,   but I

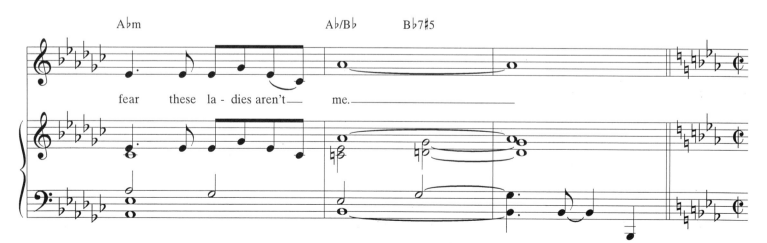

fear   these la - dies aren't___   me._____

Medium cut time

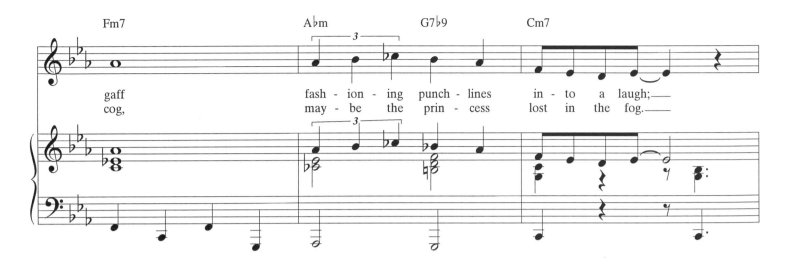

gaff / cog,
fash - ion - ing punch - lines in - to a laugh;—
may - be the prin - cess lost in the fog.—

To Coda ⊕   *D.S. (take 2nd ending) al Coda*

too cute by half.— I don't— know, don't ask me.
Kissed the one frog— who was— worth

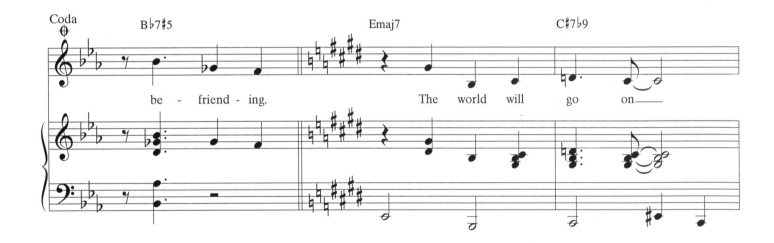

Coda ⊕

be - friend - ing. The world will go on—

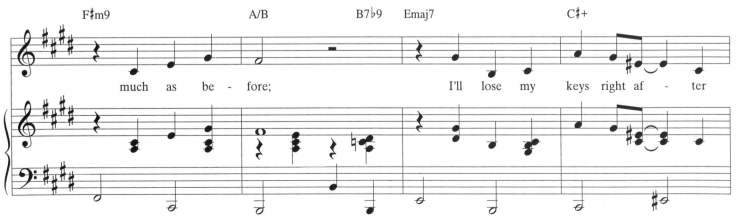

much as be - fore; I'll lose my keys right af - ter

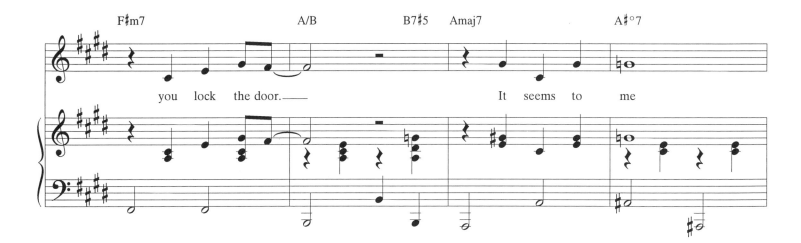

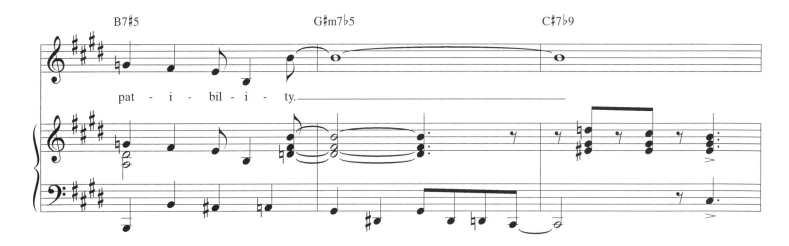

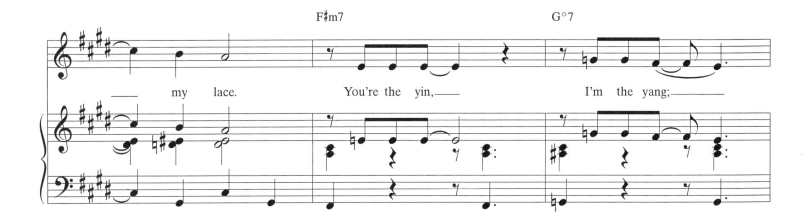

F#m7 G°7

_____ my lace. You're the yin,_____ I'm the yang;_____

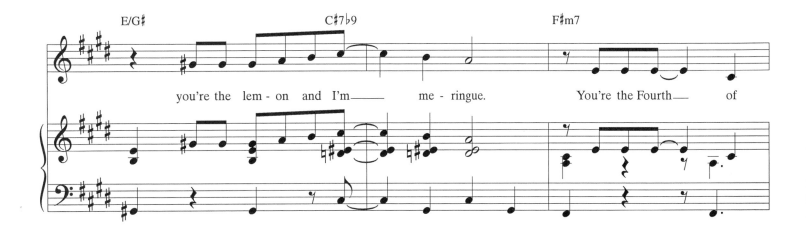

E/G# C#7♭9 F#m7

you're the lem-on and I'm_____ me-ringue. You're the Fourth_____ of

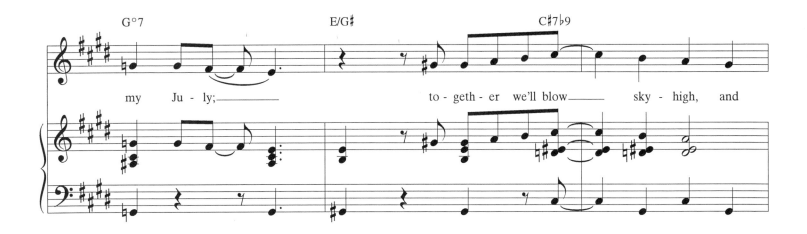

G°7 E/G# C#7♭9

my Ju-ly;_____ to-geth-er we'll blow_____ sky-high, and

F#m7 B7#5 G#m7♭5

we'll nev-er say_____ good-bye._____

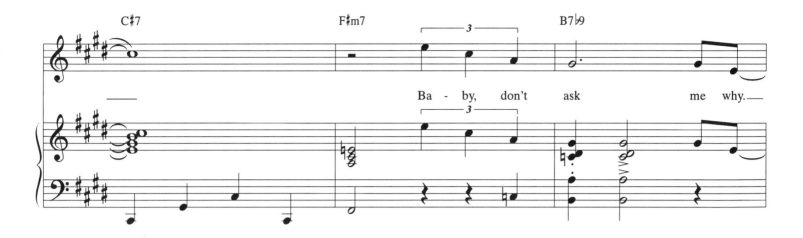

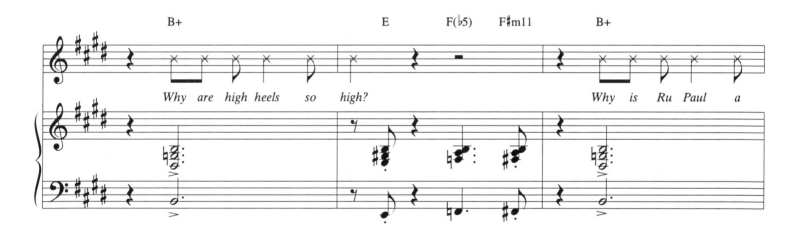

Over The Rainbow

Music by Harold Arlen
Words by E.Y. Harburg

Cm7add4   A♭7   B♭maj7   G7♭9   C7   F7sus4

and the dreams that you dare to dream real-ly do come

B♭maj7   B♭6/F   E♭/F

true. Some-day I'll wish up-on a star and wake up where the clouds are far be-

B♭6/F   E♭/F   B♭maj7

hind me._____ Where trou-bles melt like lem-on drops, a-

A7sus4   A7   Dm   A7/C♯   Cm7   B9♯5

way, a-bove the chim-ney tops; that's where you'll find me.

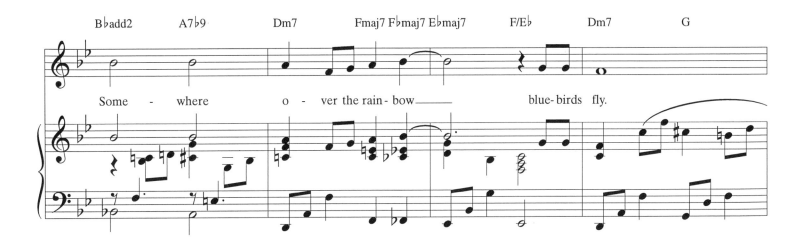

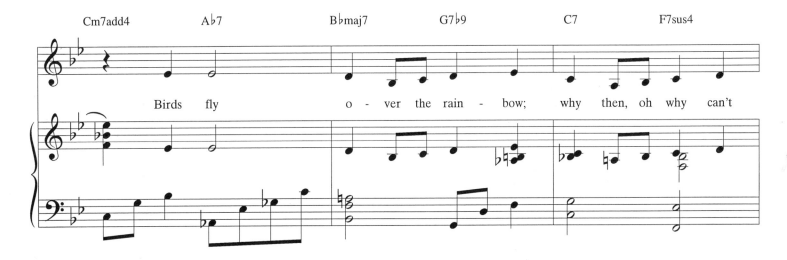

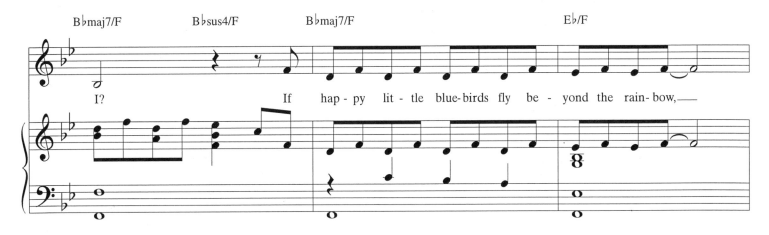

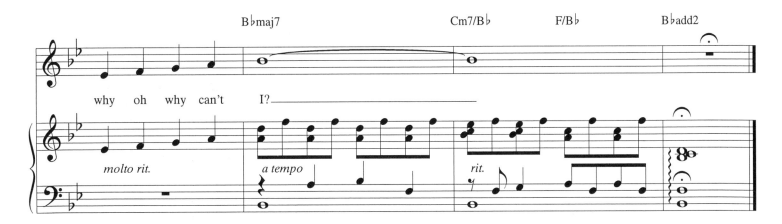

Big Time

Words by Jack Murphy
Music by Frank Wildhorn

Fast Swing

He said, "You've got the goods to make the ___ big time," ___
Be - fore you know it I was mov - in' ___ up there, ___

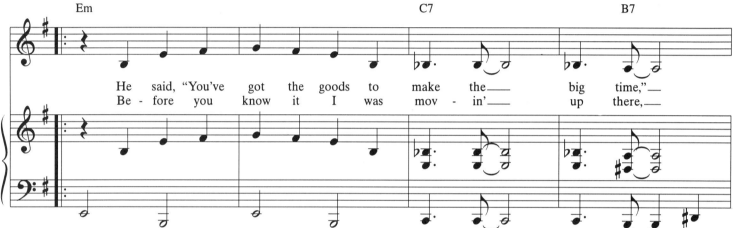

and then he puffed on his ci - gar. ___
Dom Per - ig - non and cav - i - ar. ___

We'll make a kill - ing, ___ you'll get top bill - ing. ___
A late - night "yes sir" ___ leads to good press, sir, ___

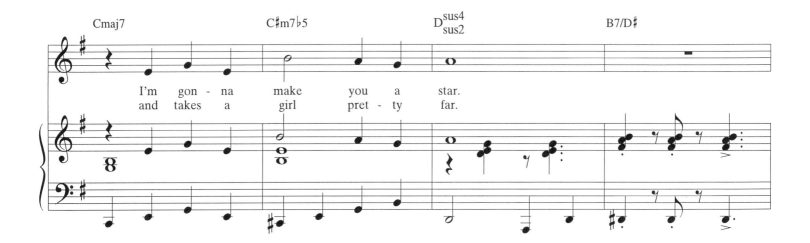

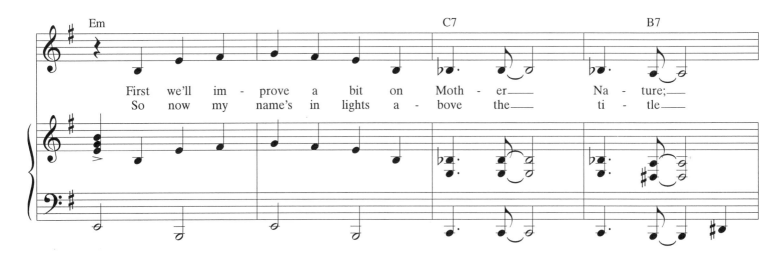

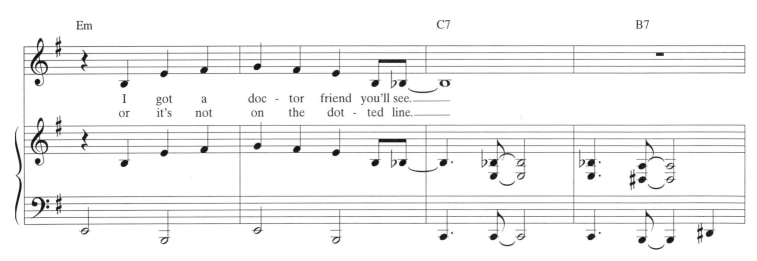

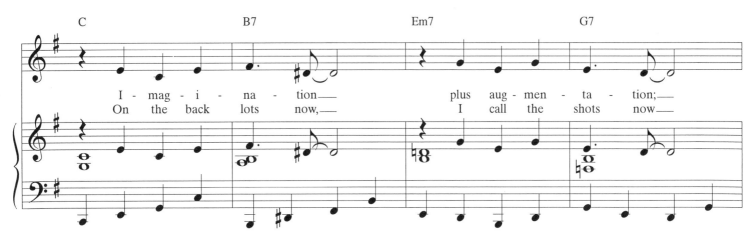

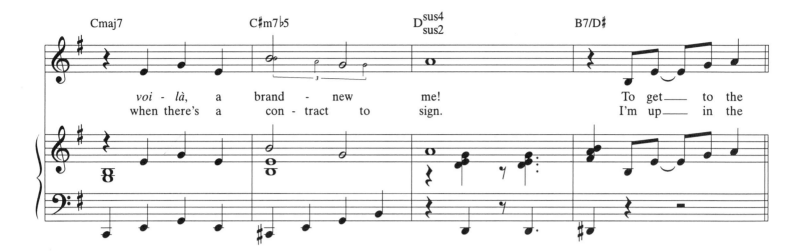

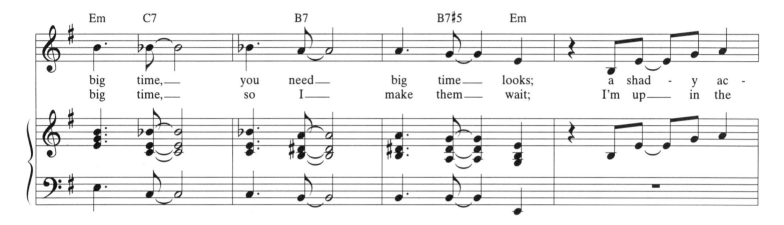

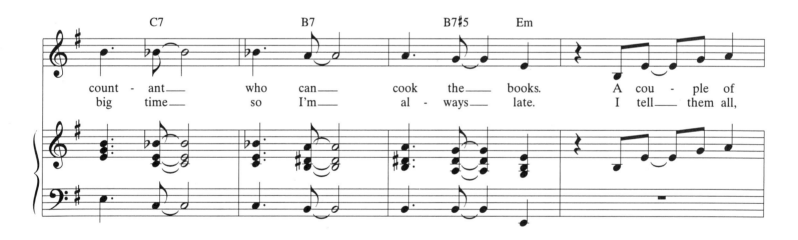

reap those big time_____ div - i - dends._____

big - brass, first - class,_____ big - time bunch.__

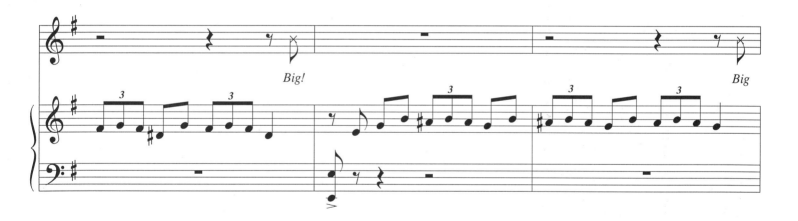

Big!

time!

Big

*Big time gig!*_____

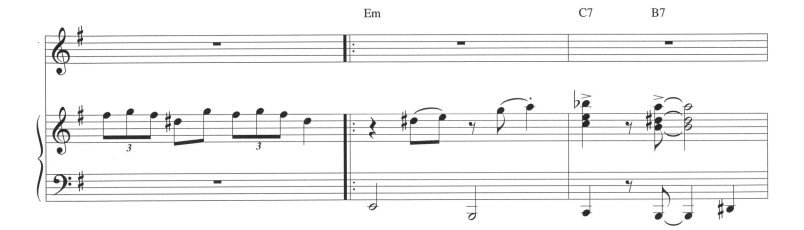

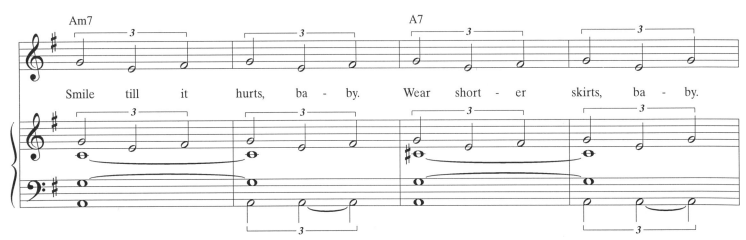

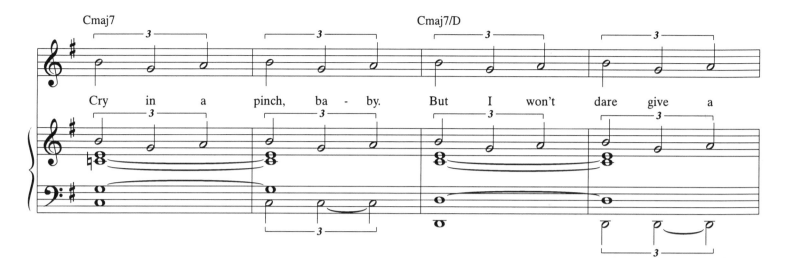

Cry in a pinch, ba - by. But I won't dare give a

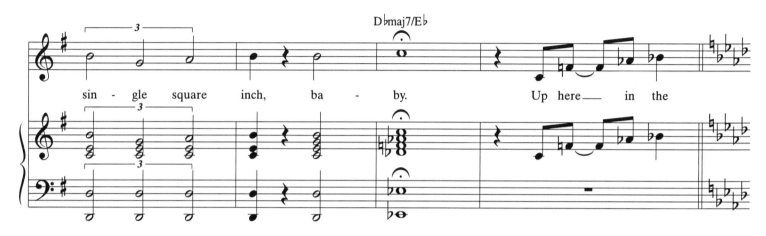

sin - gle square inch, ba - by. Up here — in the

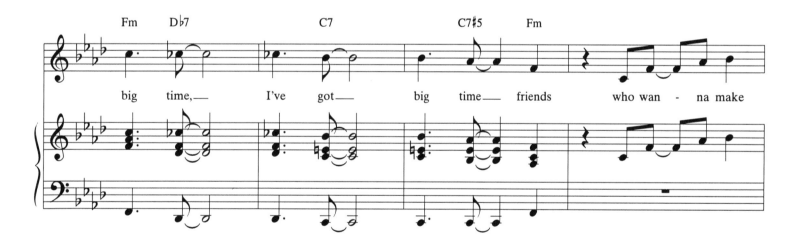

big time, — I've got — big time — friends who wan - na make

sure my — big time — nev - er — ends. My mot - to is

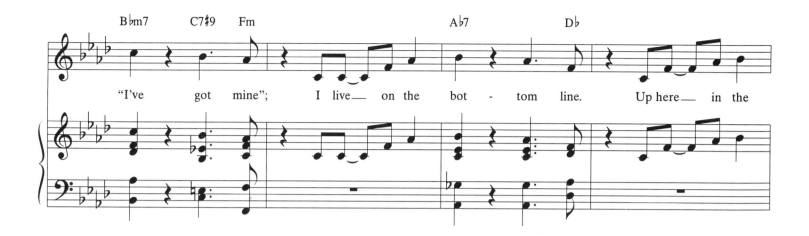

"I've got mine"; I live— on the bot - tom line. Up here— in the

A - team, wet - dream,—— big, big time!—

It's com - in' up ros - es—— and Bar - ry-more nos - es.—

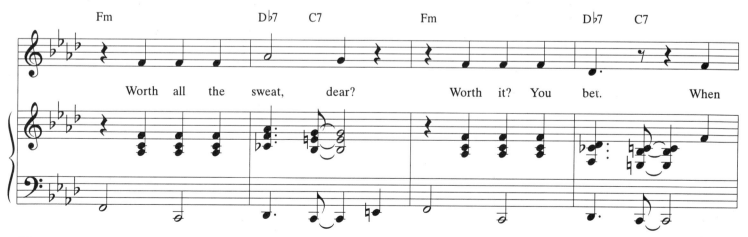

Worth all the sweat, dear? Worth it? You bet. When

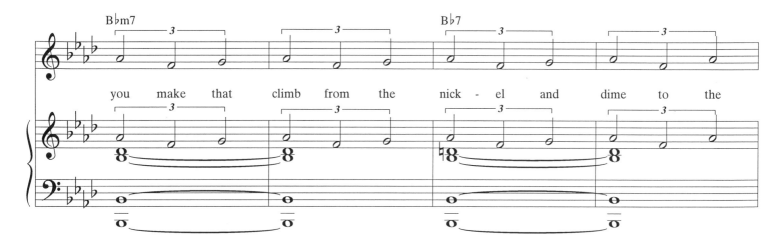

you make that climb from the nick - el and dime to the

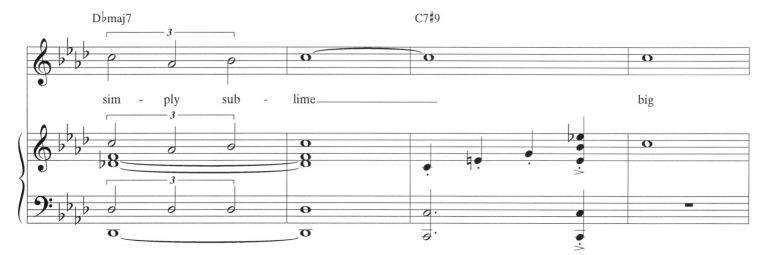

sim - ply sub - lime_____ big

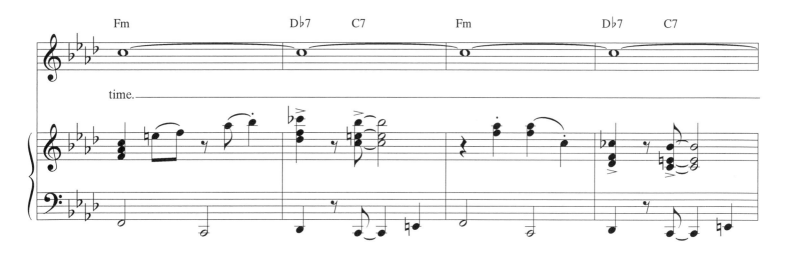

time._____

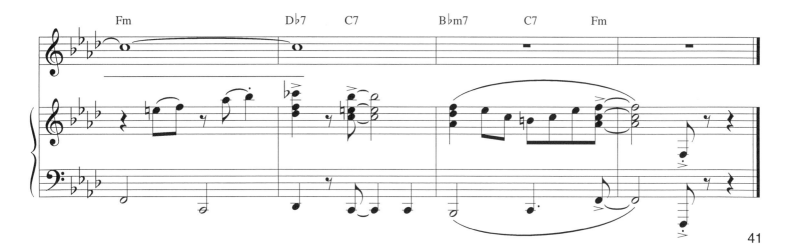

When Autumn Comes

Words by Jack Murphy
Music by Frank Wildhorn

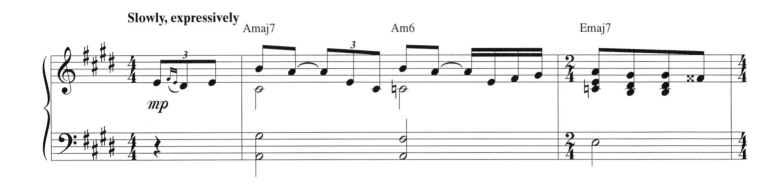

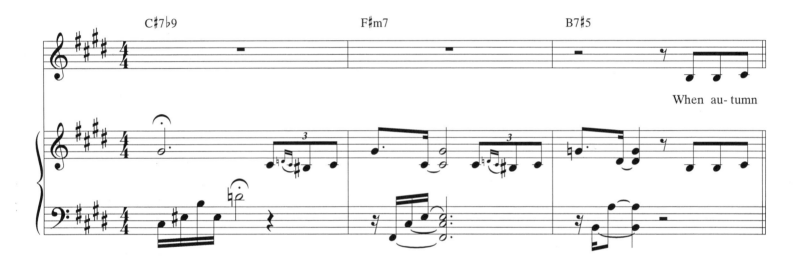

When au-tumn

comes   and leaves o - bey,   I think of   you when spring was new and fall was

comes   and wild geese fly,   I won-der   do you see them too a - cross the

miles a - way.
rest - less sky?

And when I close my_____ eyes, I see you and
And does Oc - to - ber_____ catch you dream - ing of

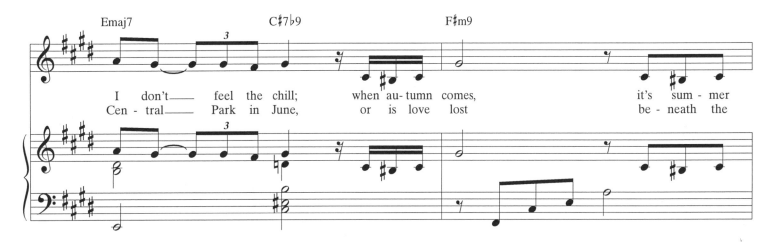

I don't_____ feel the chill;
Cen - tral_____ Park in June,

when au - tumn comes,
or is love lost

it's sum - mer
be - neath the

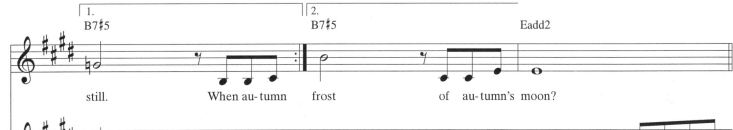

1.

2.

still.

When au - tumn frost

of au - tumn's moon?

Sum - mers by the sea

when the sun would lin - ger_____ till the

moon was high;___ days of you and me

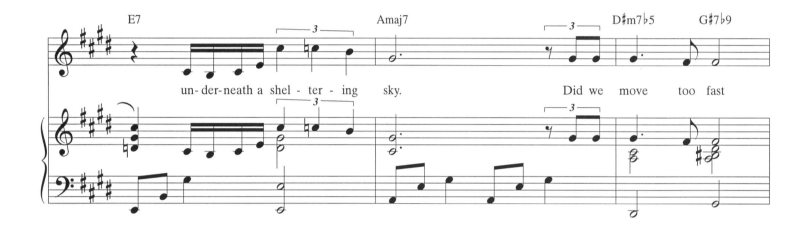

un-der-neath a shel-ter-ing sky. Did we move too fast

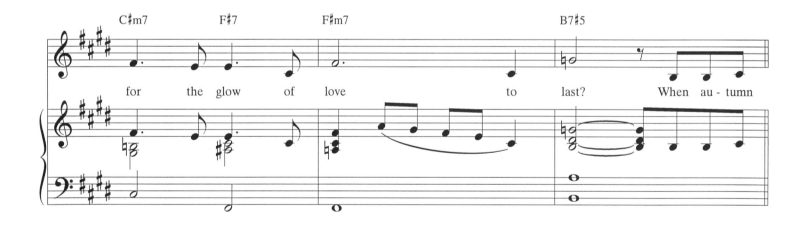

for the glow of love to last? When au-tumn

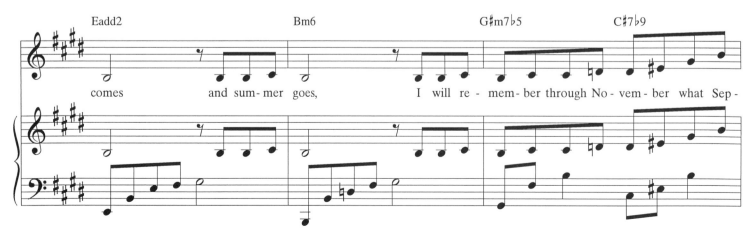

comes and sum-mer goes, I will re-mem-ber through No-vem-ber what Sep-

tem - ber knows: that noth - ing___ lasts for - ev - er and

sum - mer___ love moves on. So when the leaves be - gin to change, I find it

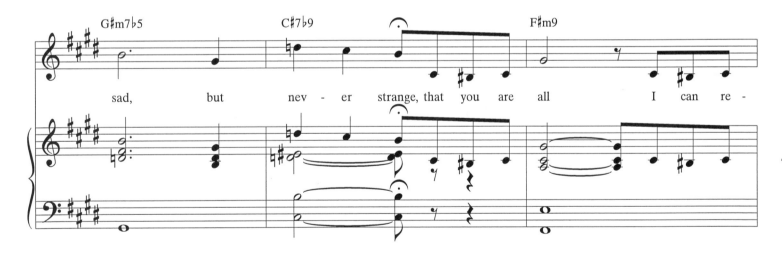

sad, but nev - er strange, that you are all I can re -

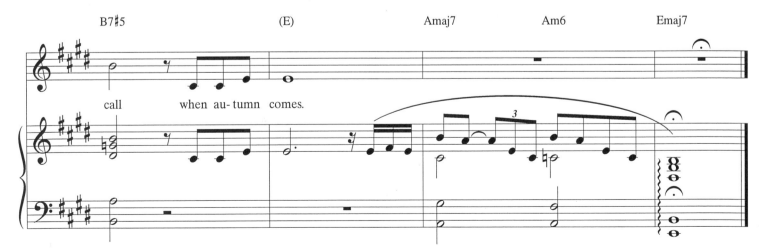

call when au - tumn comes.

Intermission—
With Linda

It's Time

Without realizing what he was doing, Frank wrote our song. With Jack's incredible lyric matching the emotional peaks and swells in the melody, "It's Time" is the epitome of a "new standard." I can only say thank you to Frank Wildhorn for writing it for me, and apologize to Frank Sinatra because it's mine.

I Want More

Frank wrote this melody and gave it to Jack, but Jack's finished lyric wasn't what Frank had in mind for the song, and he asked for a rewrite. Jack graciously agreed to try a different route. However, before discarding his work, Jack brought it to me. I read it through once and said, "Don't change a single word!". Here is a song written just for women . . . and a few men.

I'm Afraid This Must Be Love

For some reason, I feel the ghost of Fred Astaire every time I sing this song. Maybe Jack did too, and that's why he put Fred's name in the lyric. If you close your eyes while you listen maybe you can see him, as I do, gliding around the room. Sorry Fred, the song came too late. But better late . . .

Don't Ask Me Why

On my last album Frank and Jack wrote a song called "Is This Any Way To Fall In Love" and in doing so they created a character who was having trouble with her love life. I'm happy to say that she is back on two songs on this album, "I Want More" and this song. A modern woman stuck in a modern world, looking for old-fashioned love. This arrangement makes me smile every time I hear it.

Over The Rainbow

Watching Judy sing this in *The Wizard Of Oz* made something click in my nine-year-old mind. I remember sitting at my father's knee and telling him that I was going to be a singer. So now I have come full circle by recording this song. The way you hear it on the album is the way that you will hear it in my concerts. Jeremy and I recorded it late one night in the studio. It is a complete take and has some raw edges, but Jeremy and I found a groove, and rather than smooth those edges, we decided to leave the integrity of the performance alone. I hope Harold Arlen and Yip Harburg would have approved.

Big Time

Being, by nature, a small-town, outdoor, hands-in-the-earth kind of person, there is a big part of me that rebels against the whole idea of "show business." The business part is the necessary evil price I pay for the magic moments when I'm actually making the music. But just because I pay it doesn't mean I can't complain about it . . . loudly.

When Autumn Comes

Lyrics do many things, but the really good ones create images. The lyrics in this song paint portraits—poignant, sad, haunting pictures that are married to this gorgeous melody like the sun is to the moon: perfect and timeless.

Linda's comments reprinted from the liner notes to the Atlantic recording.

Man Of La Mancha (I, Don Quixote)

I want to thank my friend Colm Wilkinson for giving me the inspiration to sing this song. It was only after hearing his great rendition that I said "All right . . . I don't care if it was written for a man . . . I have to sing this song!" I did, and I'm still singing it in every concert and always having a blast.

I Don't Know How To Say Goodbye

The team of Wildhorn/Murphy strikes again. I don't know where Frank got his idea for this melody, but I do know where Jack got his idea for the lyric. At the funeral of a family member, he looked into the despairing eyes of the man's widow. What he saw there must have haunted him. I must say that I take little credit for the magic of this track. It really belongs to Frank, Jack and to Jeremy for his incredible piano work.

Candle In The Window

I feel very honored to be part of such an important album as *The Civil War: An American Musical* and to record my part of it alongside so many of today's top country, pop, Broadway and classical artists. "Candle In The Window" is different from anything I have previously recorded and there is something special and hypnotic about it. It just sweeps you along and keeps rolling. You don't want it to stop. So, though it is part of the *Civil War* album, we couldn't resist adding it.

Last Tango

I bow down to the brilliant musicians on this track. It was an honor and a privilege to sing with them. The vocal is unnecessary, the groove is paramount, but then . . . it is my album!!

Unusual Way

I've always liked this song ever since I heard it sung in an audition, but I always heard it in a slightly different way. Fortunately Jeremy soon heard it the same way and created a great track that really helps bring this version to life.

Linda Eder
It's Time

Only Love

There isn't a person alive who enjoys singing more than Frank. And very few who sing worse. But the first time Frank sang this for me, I got tears in my eyes. I have to thank Nan Knighton. It is always a pleasure to sing her lyrics, especially when they are as lovely and poetic as these.

Children Of Eve

We did the first demo of this song a while ago and it's been sitting on the shelf but never far from our minds. Frank was convinced that this song had a life. I loved the demo, but felt that I needed to sing about something a little bigger than the original lyrics. It had to say a little more in order to fit on this album. The resulting lyric is a combination of Frank, Jack and me. We tried, without wanting to preach, to make a comment on children caught in the crossfire of physical abuse, starvation, and war. If this song indeed has a life, I hope it helps those too small to defend themselves.

Something To Believe In

One of my greater worries over the last three years has been that someone else would record this song before I got the chance. It was written at the same time as the material for my last album, *And So Much More,* but it had no place on that album. I close every performance with this piece, because I like what it says, and because my soul just loves this song.

Man Of La Mancha (I, Don Quixote)

Music by Mitch Leigh
Words by Joe Darion

Moderately fast

Hear me

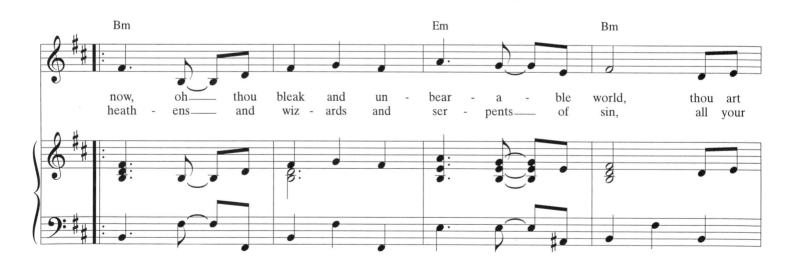

now, oh— thou bleak and un - bear - a - ble world, thou art
heath - ens— and wiz - ards and ser - pents— of sin, all your

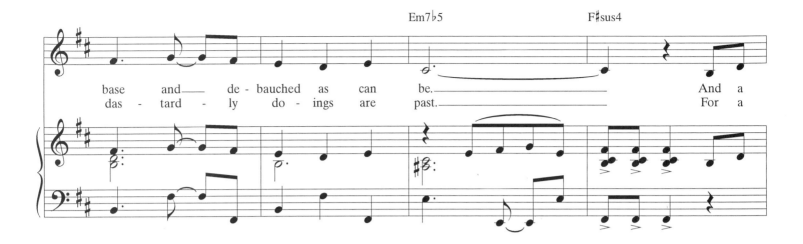

base and— de-bauched as can be.——— And a
das-tard-ly do-ings are past.——— For a

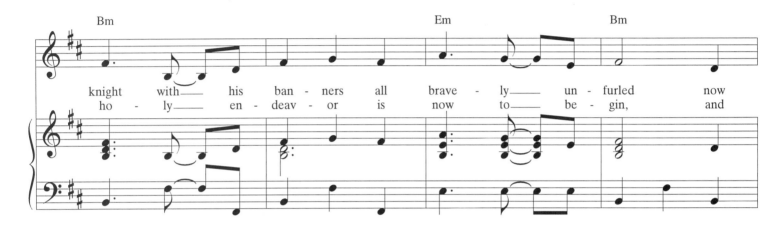

knight with— his ban-ners all brave-ly— un-furled now
ho-ly— en-deav-or is now to— be-gin, and

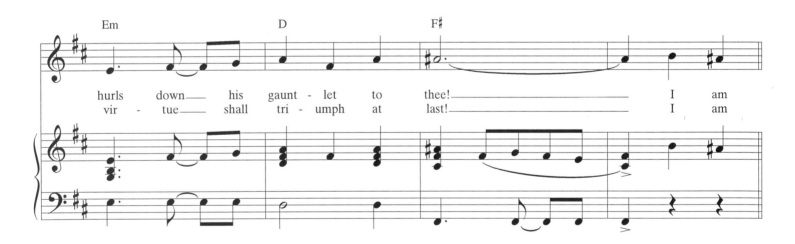

hurls down— his gaunt-let to thee!——— I am
vir-tue— shall tri-umph at last!——— I am

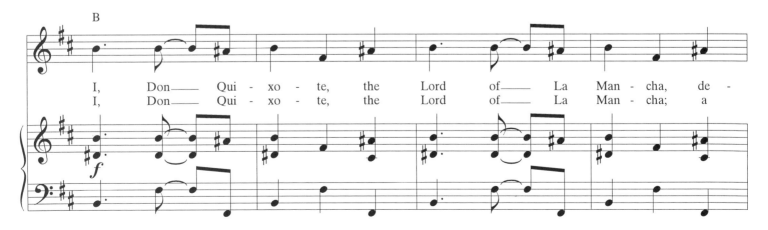

I, Don— Qui-xo-te, the Lord of— La Man-cha, de-
I, Don— Qui-xo-te, the Lord of— La Man-cha; a

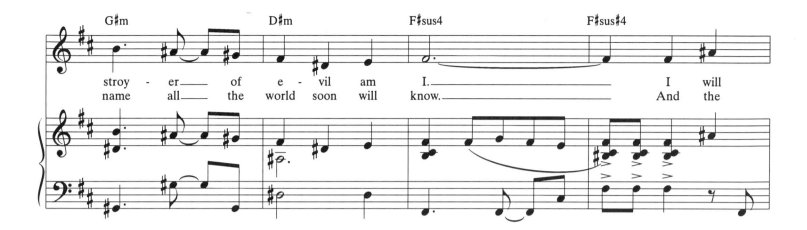

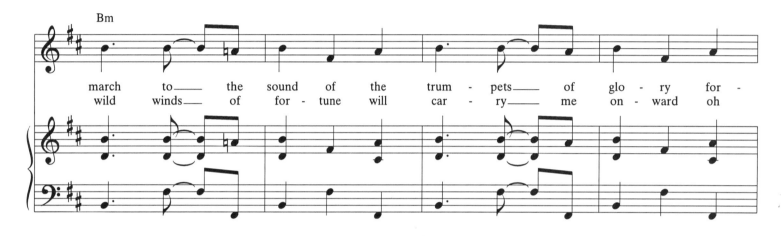

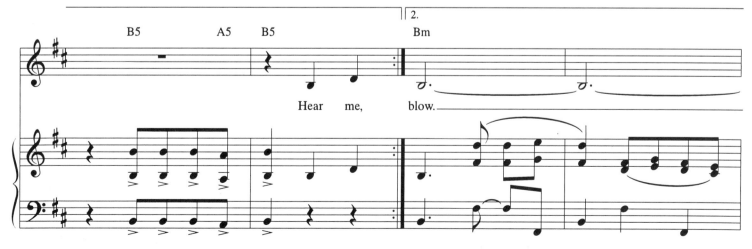

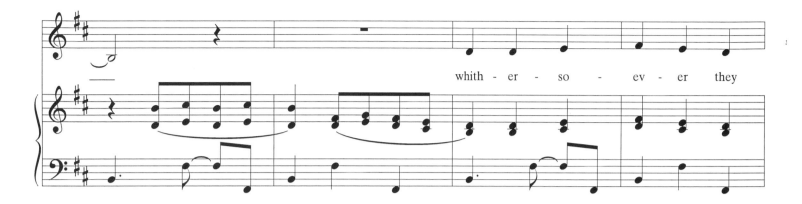

whith - er - so - ev - er they

blow. On - ward to glo - ry I

go!

I Don't Know How To Say Goodbye

Words by Jack Murphy
Music by Frank Wildhorn

Moderately slow

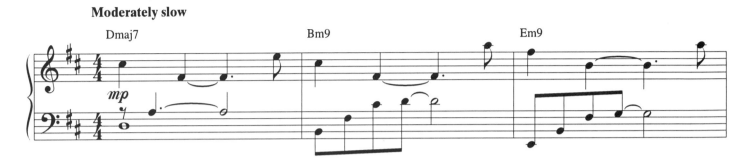

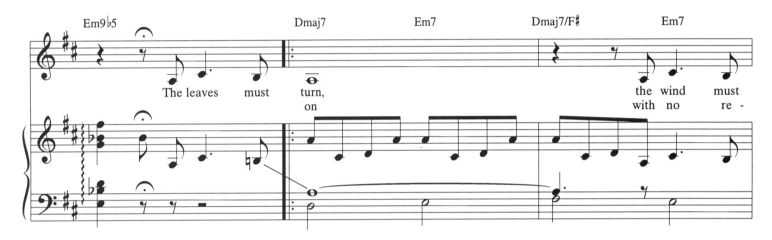

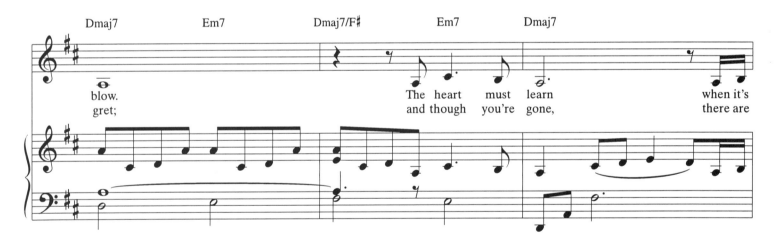

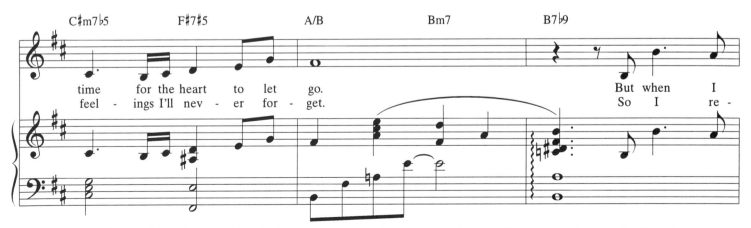

think — of you, my heart knows why
mem - ber you, and though I try,

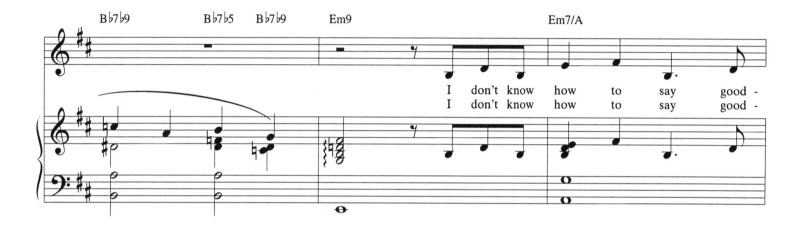

I don't know how to say good-
I don't know how to say good-

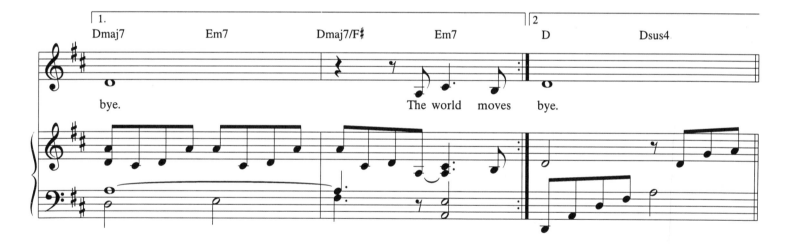

bye.

The world moves bye.

The house we used_____ to share_____ still_____

looks as if you're there._____ And I won't change a sin - gle thing,

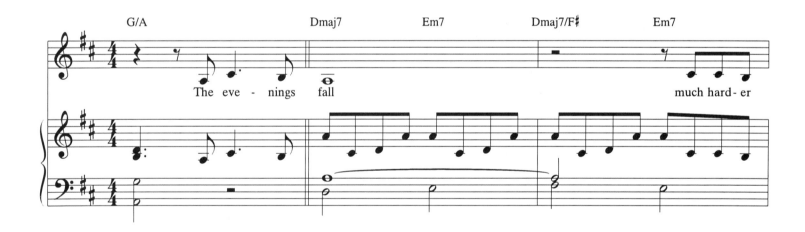

not e - ven the wed - ding ring I wear._____

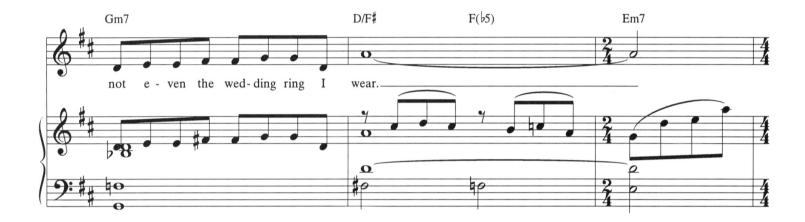

The eve - nings fall much hard - er

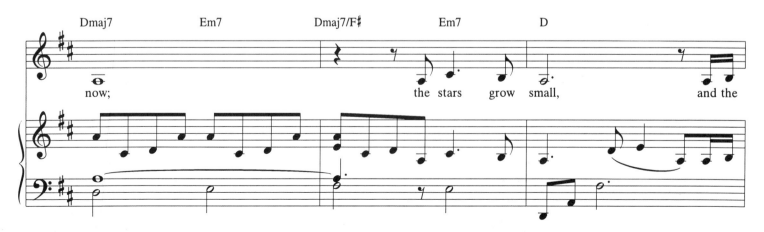

now; the stars grow small, and the

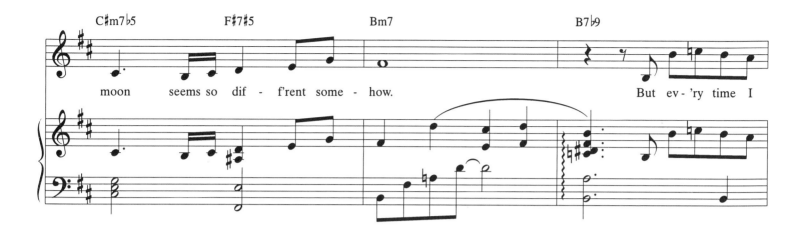

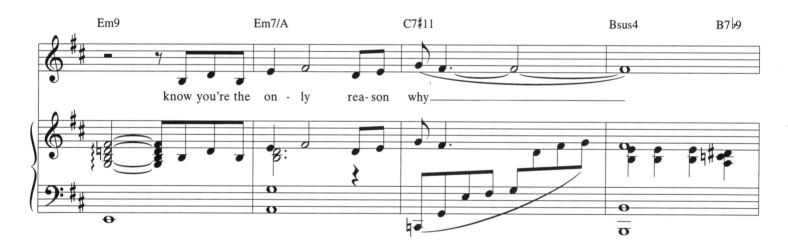

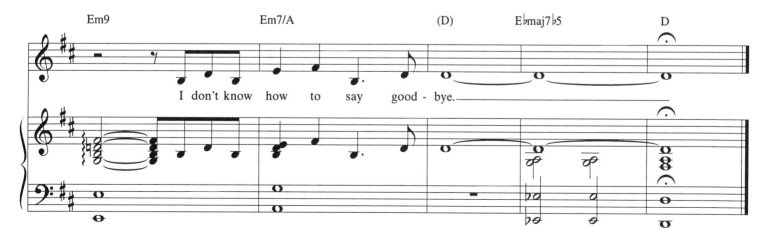

Candle In The Window

Words by Jack Murphy
Music by Frank Wildhorn

burn - ing in —— a win - dow near —— a fig - ure in a chair, ——
Ti - red of —— the de - mons, he —— must sit up there and fight, ——
he will keep —— his can - dle burn - ing just a mo - ment more, ——

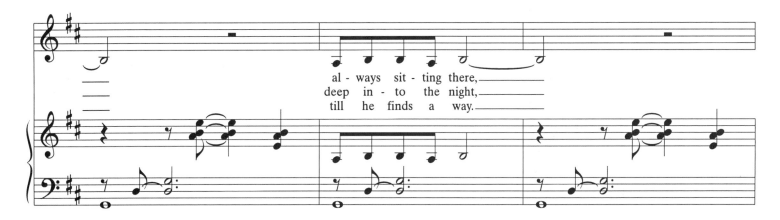

al - ways sit - ting there, ——
deep in - to the night, ——
till he finds a way. ——

1.

D6/9

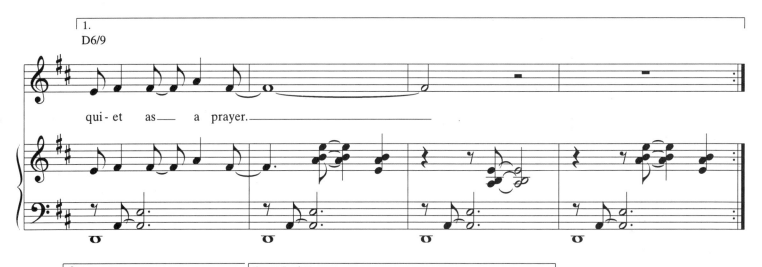

qui - et as —— a prayer. ——

2. | Omit 2nd time

D6/9

pray-ing that —— he's right. ——   Ev- 'ry
This is what —— I pray. ——   And I

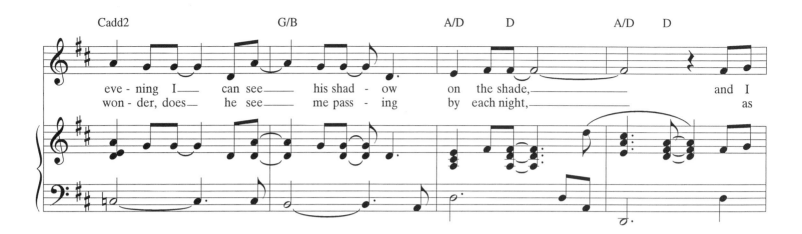

eve - ning I____ can see____ his shad - ow____ on the shade,_____ and I
won - der, does____ he see____ me pass - ing____ by each night,_____ as

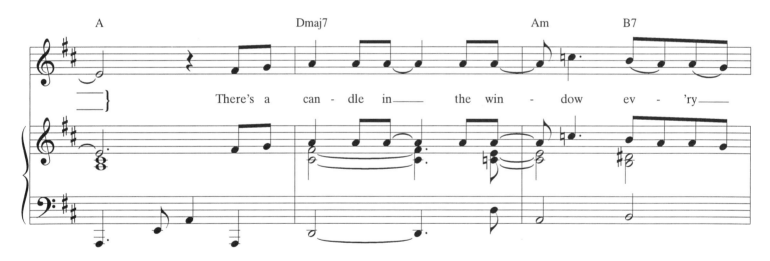

don't feel so____ a - lone____ or so____ a - fraid._____
I look up____ to find____ his patch____ of light?_____

There's a can - dle in____ the win - dow ev - 'ry____

night,____ re - flect - ing all____ our hopes and dreams,____ or

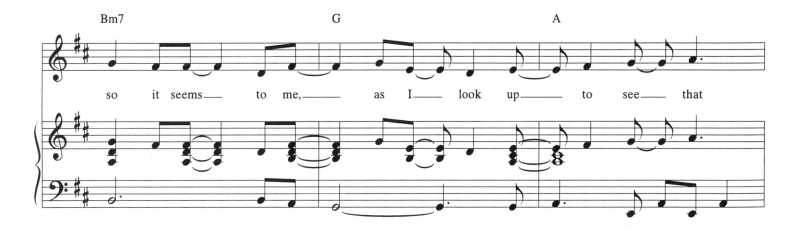

so it seems— to me,— as I— look up— to see— that

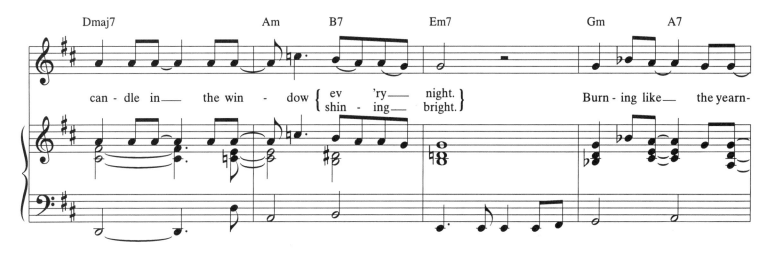

can - dle in— the win - dow { ev 'ry— night. } { shin - ing— bright. } Burn - ing like— the yearn-

A little slower

ing to— be free,— far a - way and dim,—

Tempo I

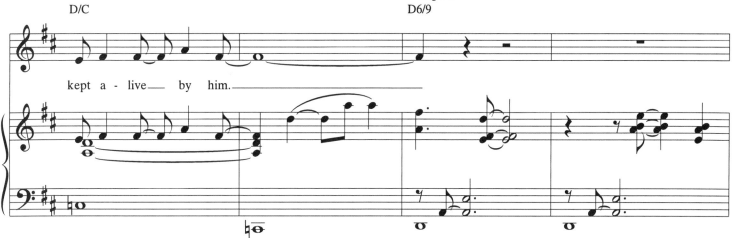

kept a - live— by him.—

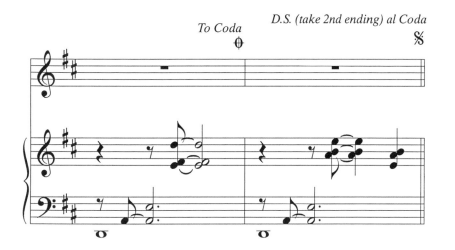

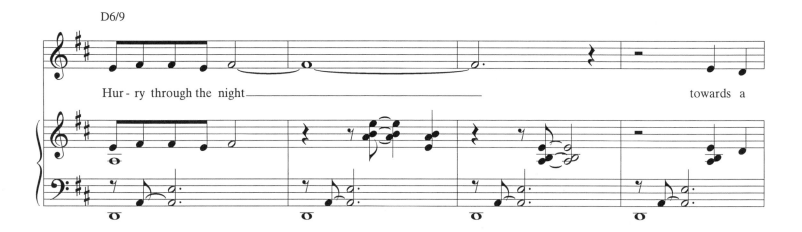

Hur - ry through the night_____ towards a

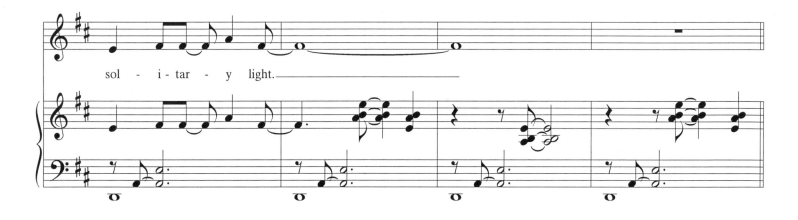

sol - i - tar - y light._____

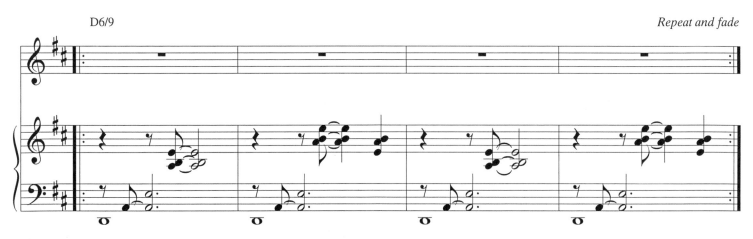

Last Tango

Words by Jack Murphy
Music by Frank Wildhorn

Moderately fast

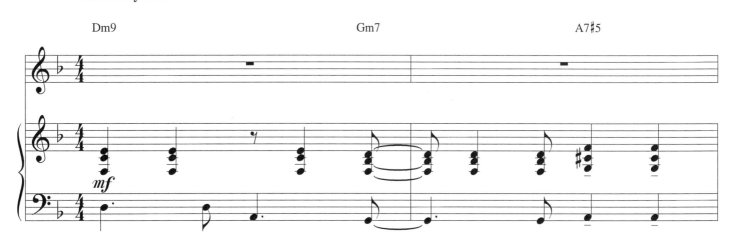

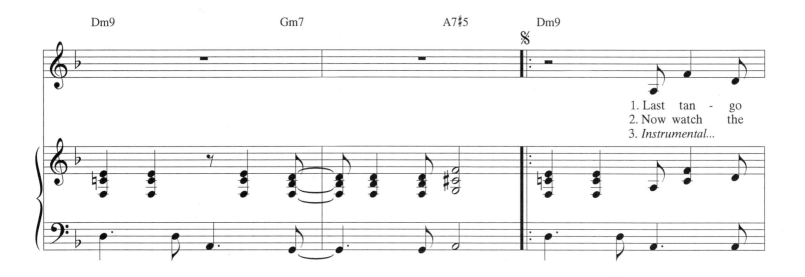

1. Last tan - go
2. Now watch the
3. *Instrumental...*

of the night,___ last song of love.
cit - y burn___ here in my eyes.

Sad mel - o - dies take flight,— cry - ing to the heav - ens a - bove.—
Down here you live and learn;— ask no ques - tions and you hear no— lies.—

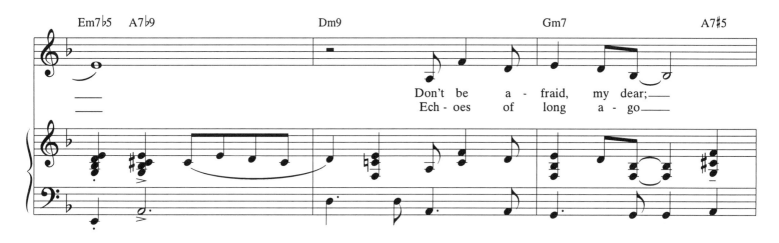

Don't be a - fraid, my dear;— you're
Ech - oes of long a - go—

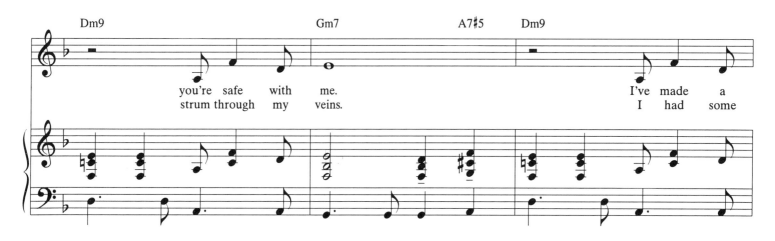

you're safe with me.
strum through my veins.

I've made a
I had some

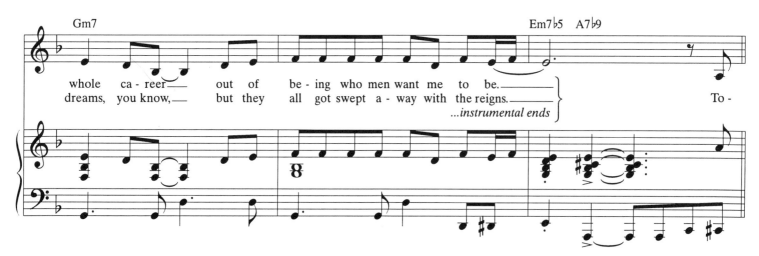

whole ca - reer— out of be - ing who men want me to be.—
dreams, you know,— but they all got swept a - way with the reigns.—

...instrumental ends

To -

night I'll make your dreams come true, but don't con-fuse this fire

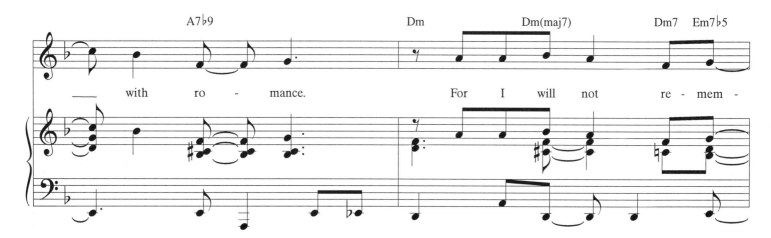

with ro - mance. For I will not re - mem -

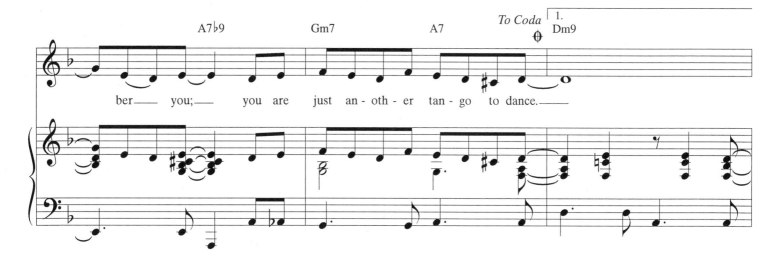

ber you; you are just an - oth - er tan - go to dance.

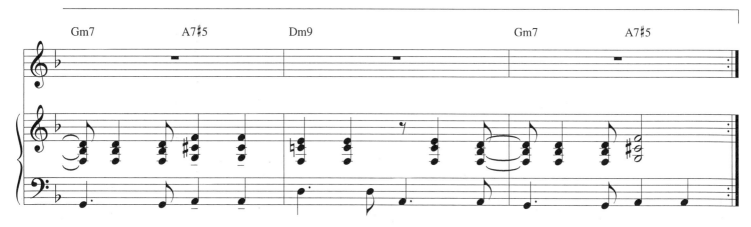

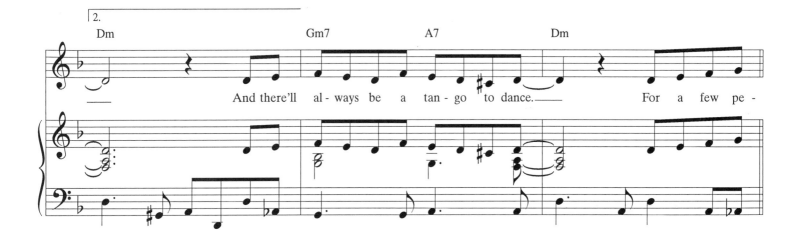

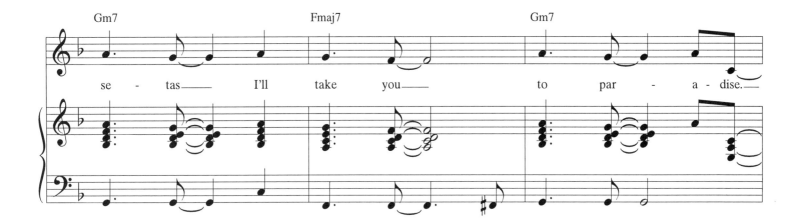

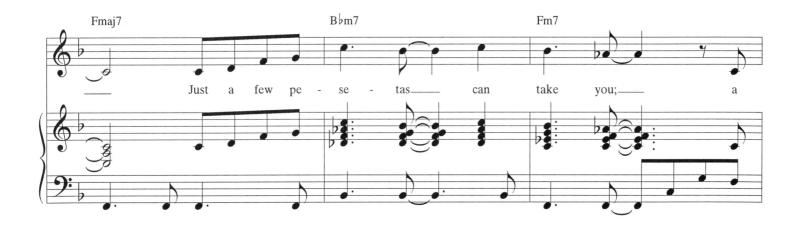

Andthere'll al-ways be a tan-go to dance.___ There will

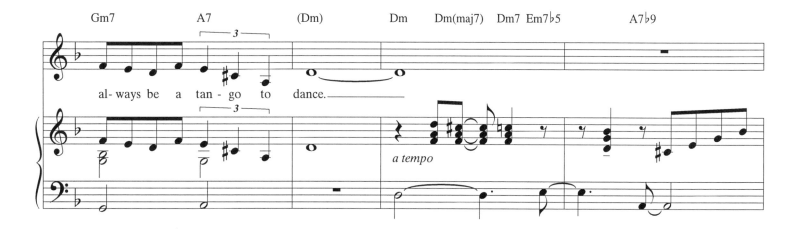

al-ways be a tan-go to dance.___

D.S. (instrumental) and fade

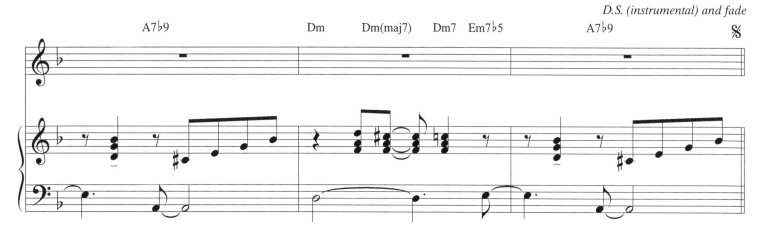

67

Unusual Way

Music and Lyrics by Maury Yeston

Moderately slow

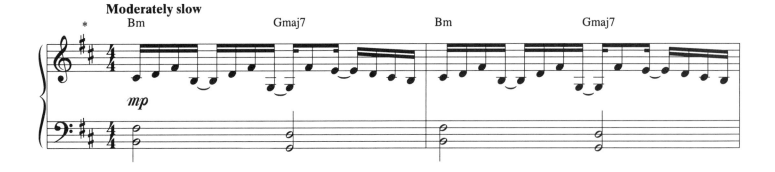

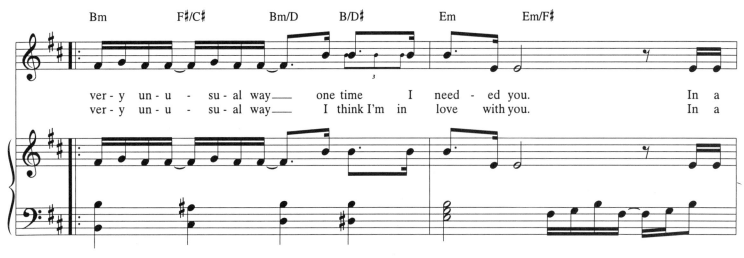

In a
ver - y un - u - su - al way ___ one time I need - ed you. In a
ver - y un - u - su - al way ___ I think I'm in love with you. In a

* Recorded a half step lower.

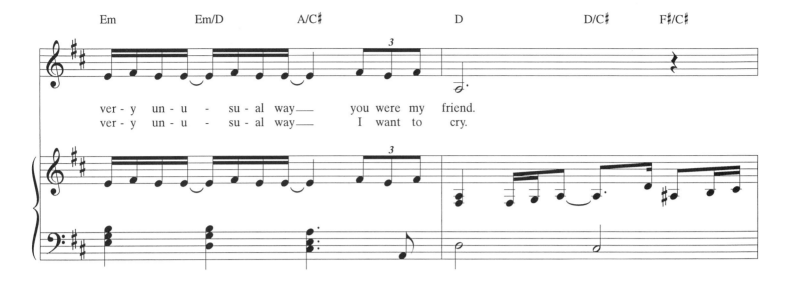

ver - y un - u - su - al way___ you were my friend.
ver - y un - u - su - al way___ I want to cry.

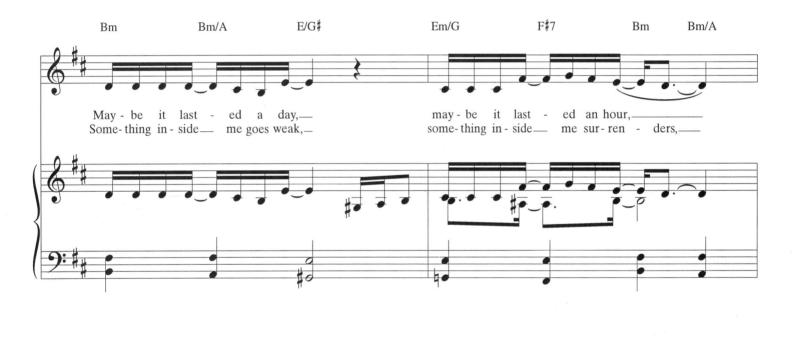

May - be it last - ed a day,___ may - be it last - ed an hour,___
Some - thing in - side___ me goes weak,___ some - thing in - side___ me sur - ren - ders,___

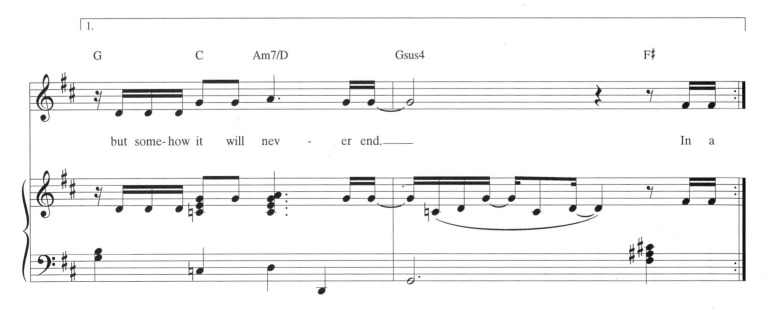

but some - how it will nev - er end.___ In a

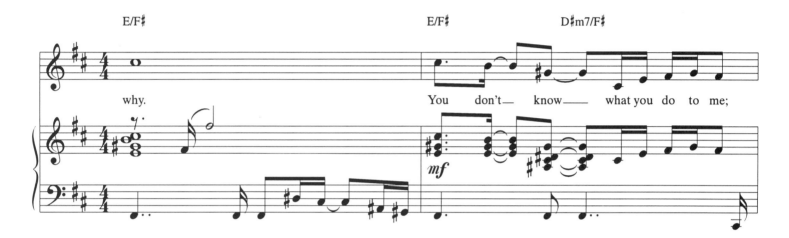

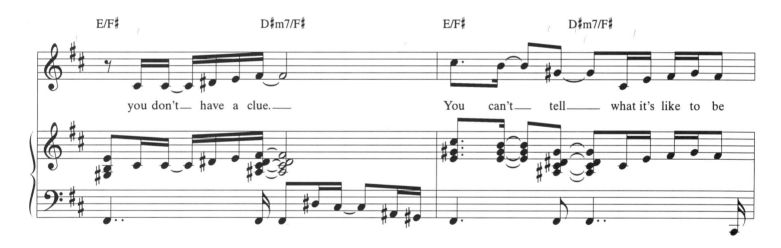

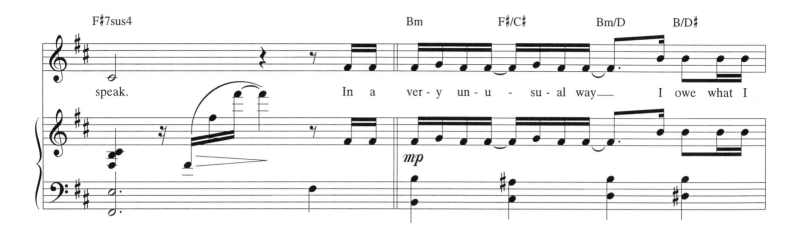

speak. In a ver-y un-u-su-al way— I owe what I

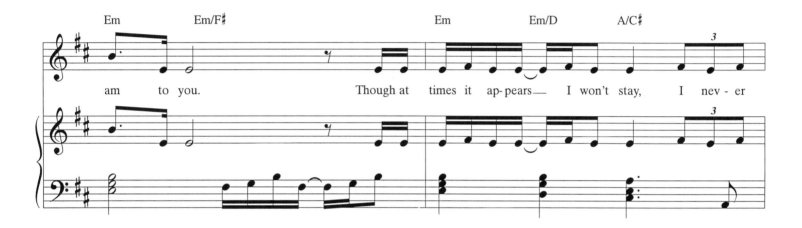

am to you. Though at times it ap-pears— I won't stay, I nev-er

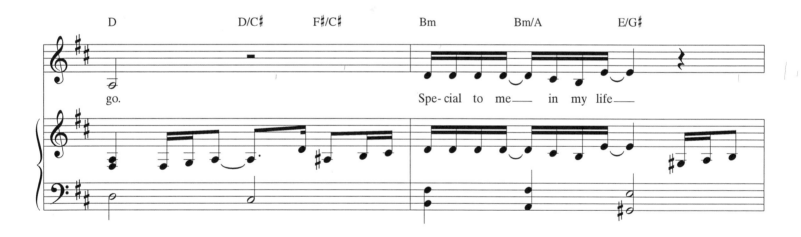

go. Spe-cial to me— in my life—

since the first day— that I met— you,— how could I ev-er for-get— you once you had touched—

71

my soul? In a

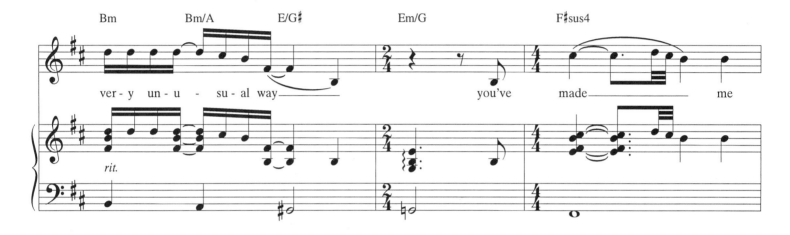

ver-y un-u-su-al way you've made me

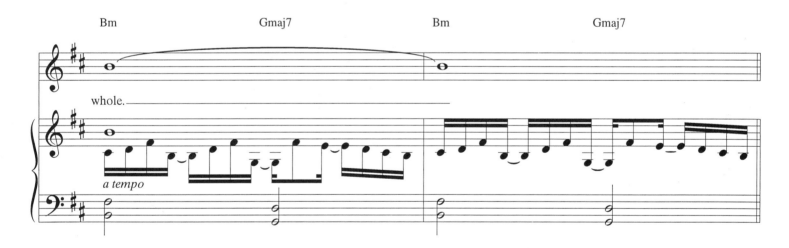

whole.

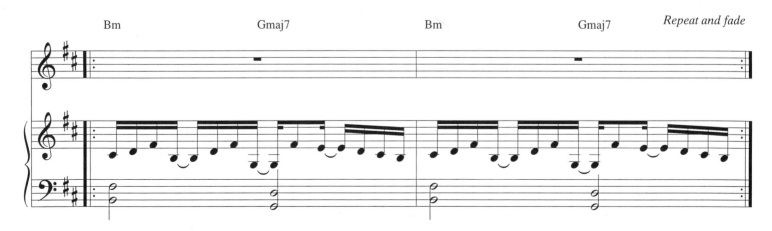

Repeat and fade

72

Something To Believe In

Music and Lyrics by Frank Wildhorn

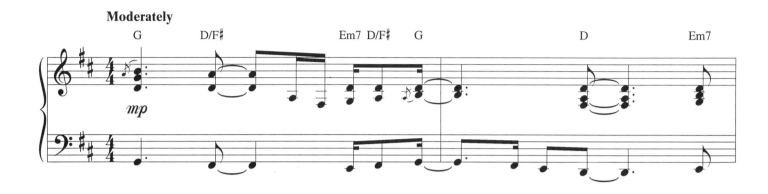

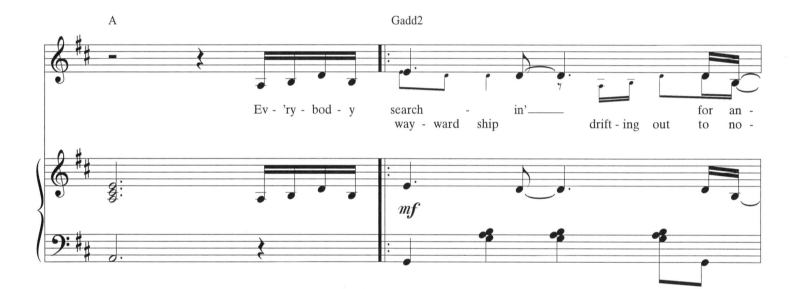

Ev - 'ry-bod - y search - in' for an-
way - ward ship drift - ing out to no -

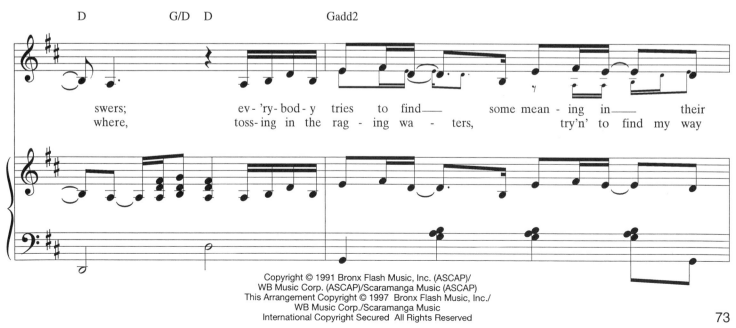

swers; ev - 'ry-bod - y tries to find some mean - ing in their
where, toss - ing in the rag - ing wa - ters, try'n' to find my way

life. _____ Where do we be - long? _____ Who will be our
home. _____ You must be an an - gel _____ watch - in'

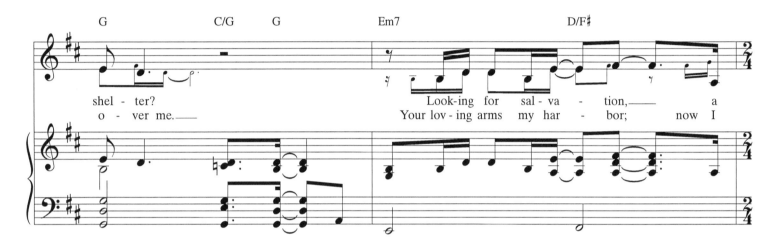

shel - ter? Look-ing for sal - va - tion, ____ a
o - ver me. ____ Your lov-ing arms my har - bor; now I

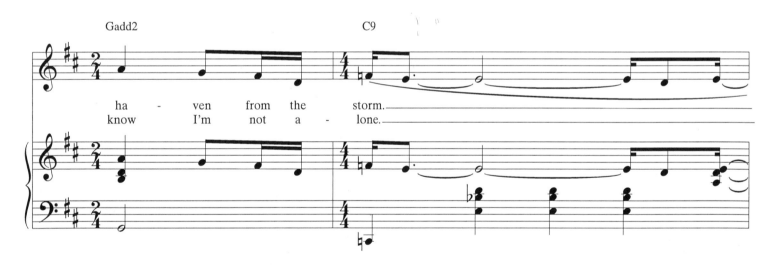

ha - ven from the storm. _____
know I'm not a - lone. _____

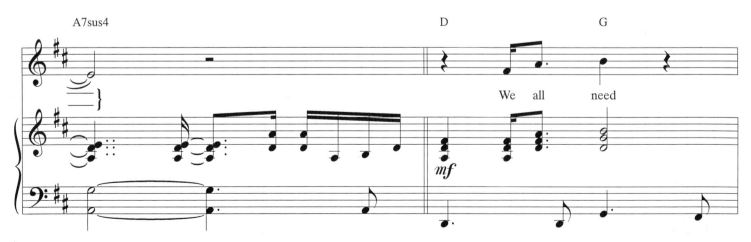

We all need

mf

74

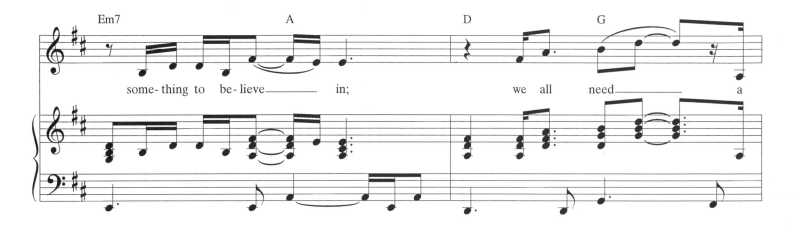

some-thing to be-lieve___ in;   we all need___ a

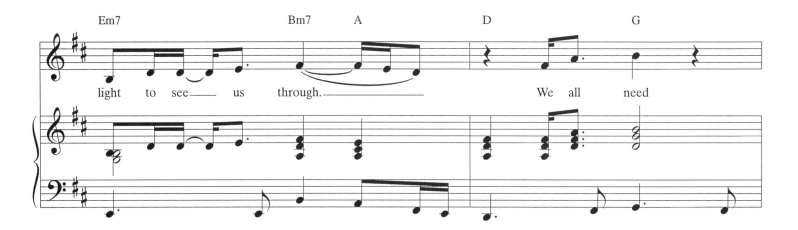

light to see___ us through.___   We all need

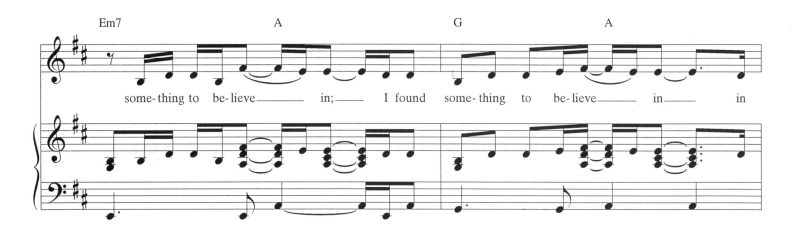

some-thing to be-lieve___ in;___ I found some-thing to be-lieve___ in___ in

you.   I was like a

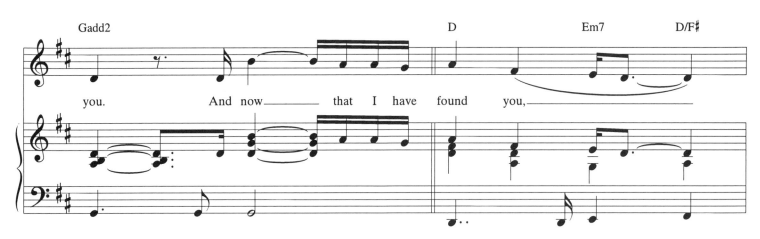

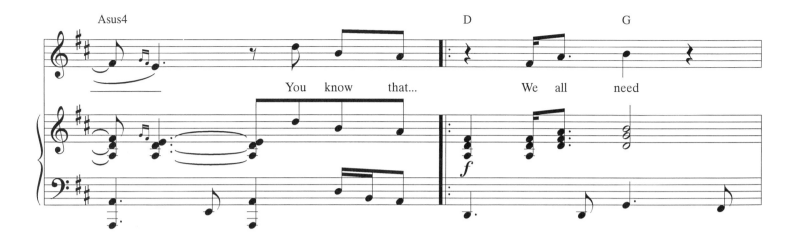

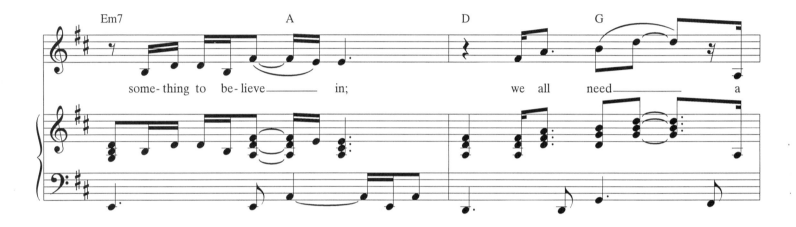

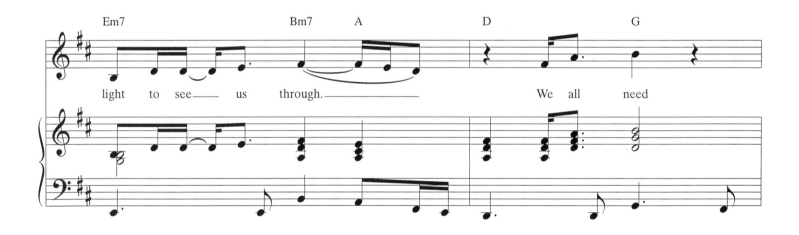

Repeat and fade

Only Love

Words by Nan Knighton
Music by Frank Wildhorn

Moderately

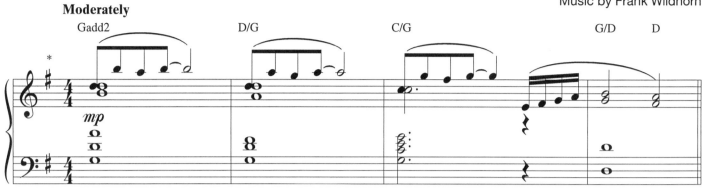

I see you try——— to turn a - way;
Come meet my eyes——— one mo - ment more;
We touch, the dark——— be - gins to stir;

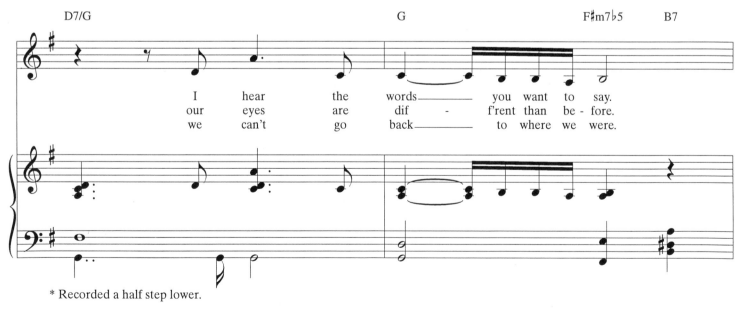

I hear the words——— you want to say.
our eyes are dif - f'rent than be - fore.
we can't go back——— to where we were.

* Recorded a half step lower.

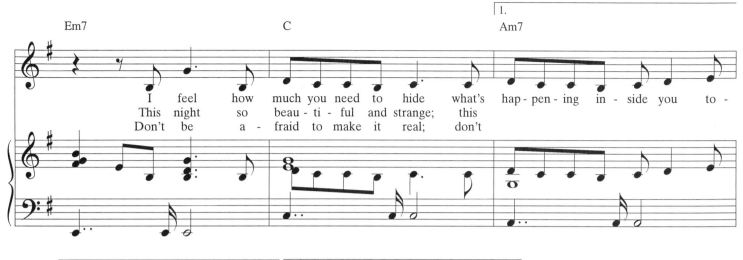

I feel how much you need to hide; what's hap-pen-ing in-side you to-
This night so beau-ti-ful and strange; this
Don't be a - fraid to make it real; don't

night.
night be - gins to change who we are. Don't
be a - fraid to feel_____ to - night. Don't

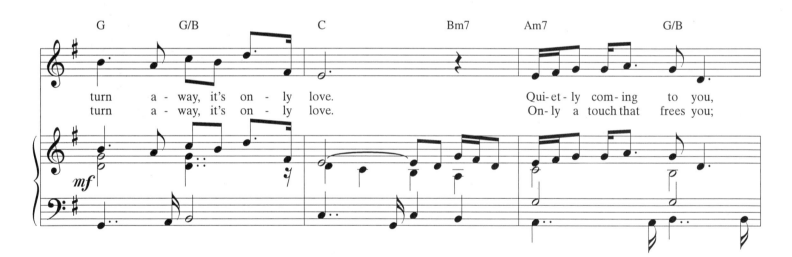

turn a - way, it's on - ly love.
turn a - way, it's on - ly love. Qui-et-ly com-ing to you,
On-ly a touch that frees you;

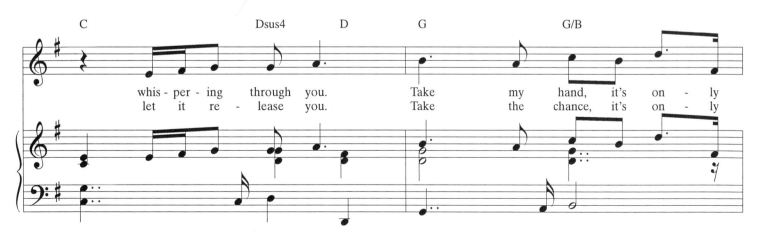

whis - per - ing through you. Take my hand, it's on - ly
let it re - lease you. Take the chance, it's on - ly

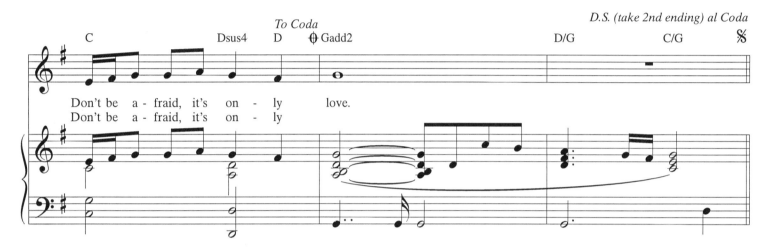

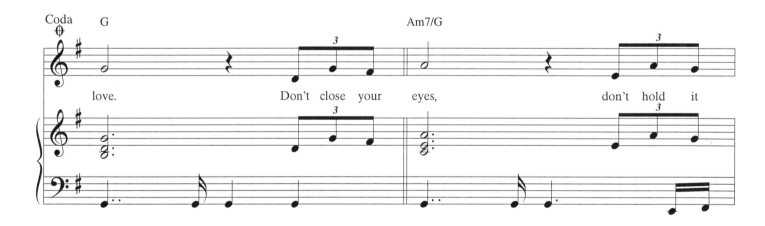

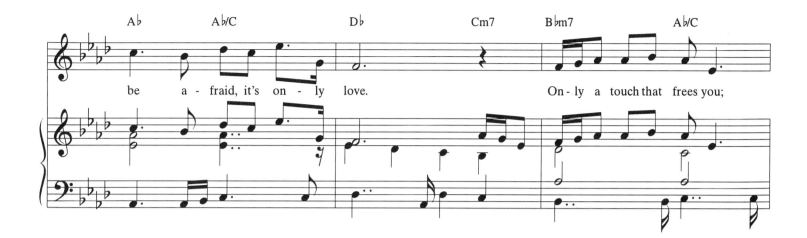

be a - fraid, it's on - ly love. On - ly a touch that frees you;

let it re - lease you. Take the chance, it's on - ly love.

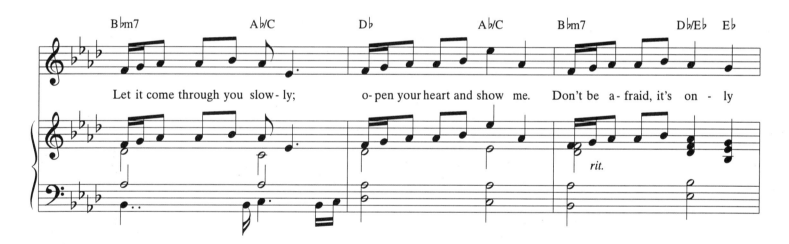

Let it come through you slow - ly; o - pen your heart and show me. Don't be a - fraid, it's on - ly

rit.

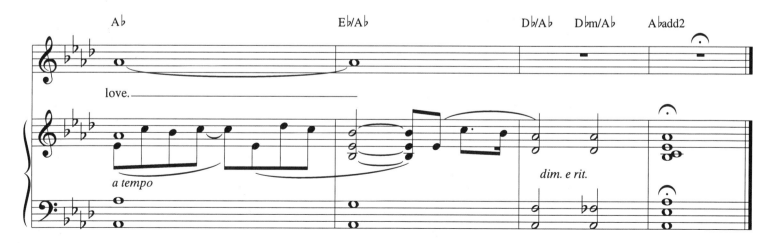

love.

a tempo *dim. e rit.*

Children Of Eve

Words by Jack Murphy and Linda Eder
Music by Frank Wildhorn

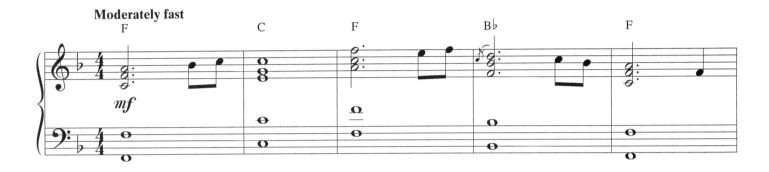

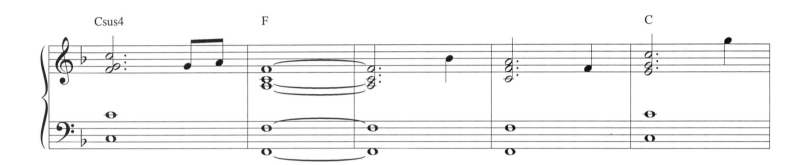

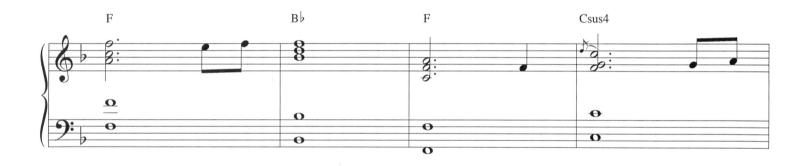

Don't

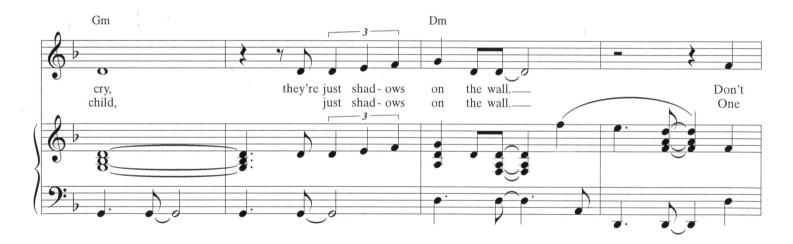

chil - dren—— of Eve sleep - ing some - where—— to -
chil - dren—— of Eve sleep—— in peace ev - 'ry
chil - dren—— of Eve sleep - ing some - where—— to -

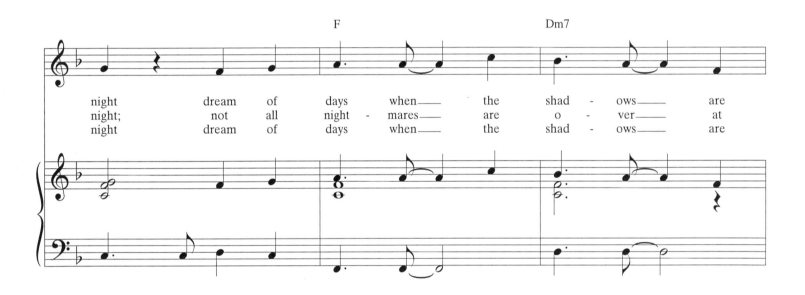

night dream of days when—— the shad - ows—— are
night; not all night - mares—— are o - ver—— at
night dream of days when—— the shad - ows—— are

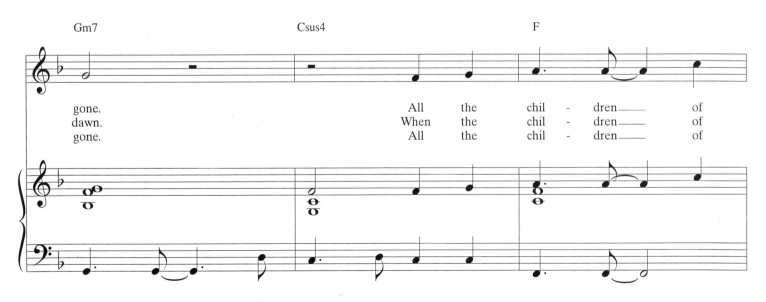

gone. All the chil - dren—— of
dawn. When the chil - dren—— of
gone. All the chil - dren—— of

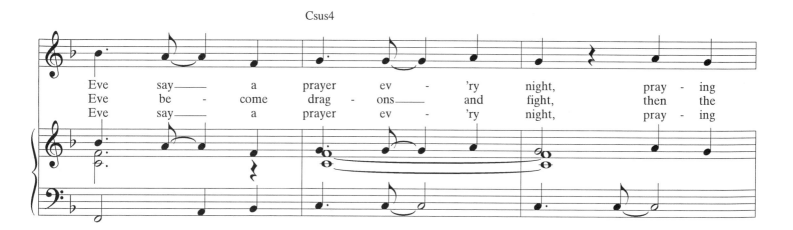

Csus4

Eve say——— a prayer ev - 'ry night, pray - ing
Eve be - come drag - ons——— and fight, then the
Eve say——— a prayer ev - 'ry night, pray - ing

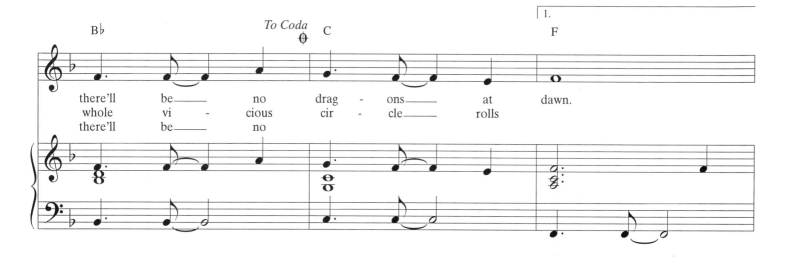

Bb   *To Coda* ⊕   C   ⌐1.   F

there'll be——— no drag - ons——— at dawn.
whole vi - cious cir - cle——— rolls
there'll be——— no

C   F   Bb

F   Csus4   F

One

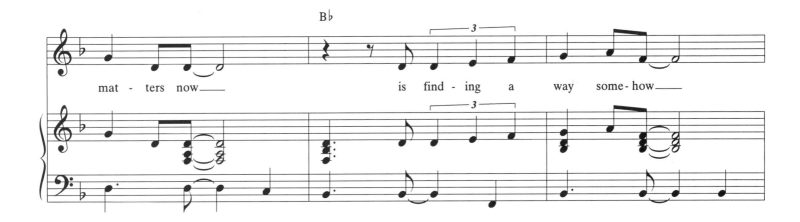

day) I'll try to be there for you_____ till there are no

D.S. al Coda

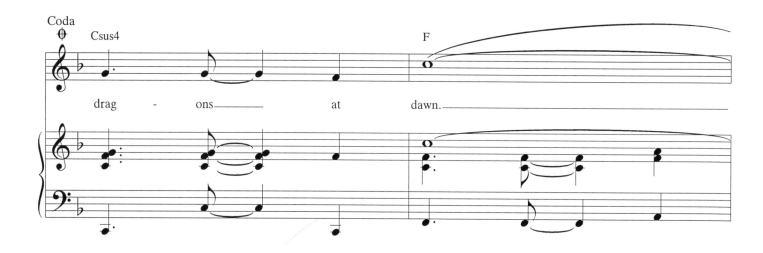

drag - ons_____ in the sky._____ All the

Coda

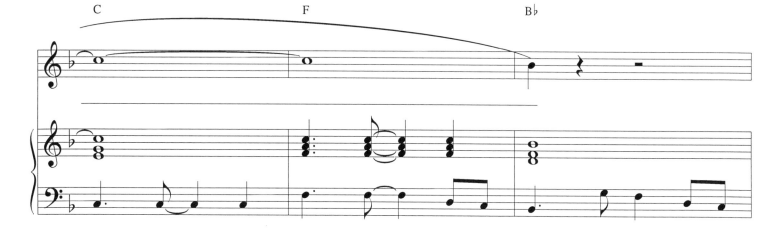

drag - ons_____ at dawn._____

We are ___ the chil - dren ___ of Eve.

We are the chil - dren. ___ Na na na na na,

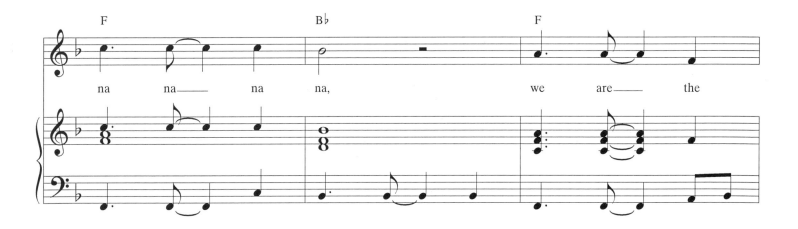

na na ___ na na, we are ___ the

Repeat and fade

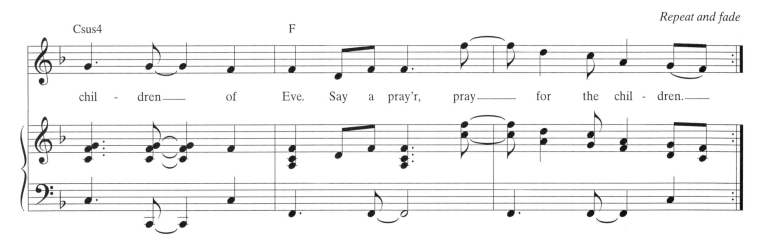

chil - dren ___ of Eve. Say a pray'r, pray ___ for the chil - dren.

Someone Like You

Words by Leslie Bricusse
Music by Frank Wildhorn

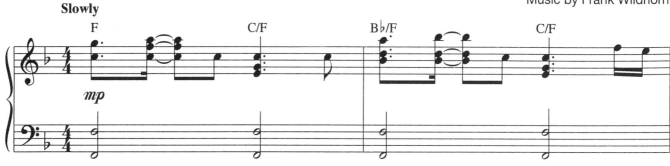

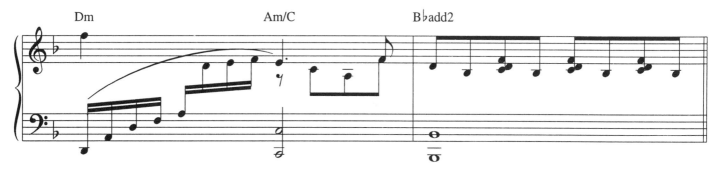

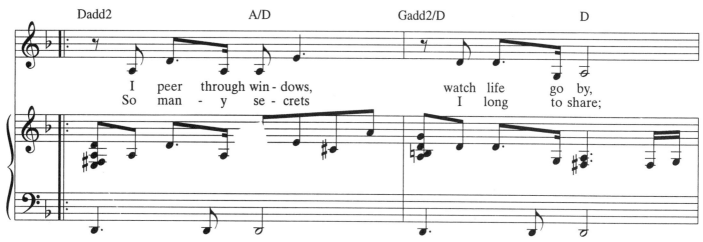

I peer through win - dows, watch life go by,
So man - y se - crets I long to share;

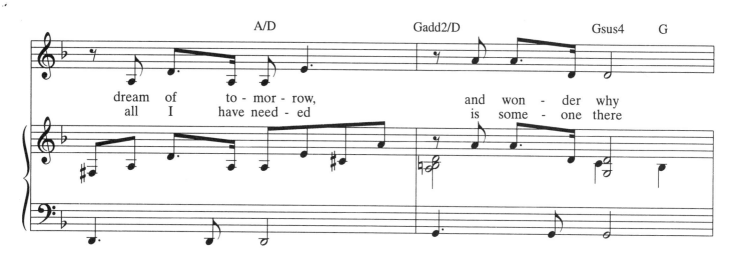

dream of to - mor - row, and won - der why
all I have need - ed is some - one there

the past is hold-ing me, keeping life at bay. I wan-der, lost in yes-ter-
to help me see a world I've nev-er seen be-fore, a love to o-pen ev-'ry

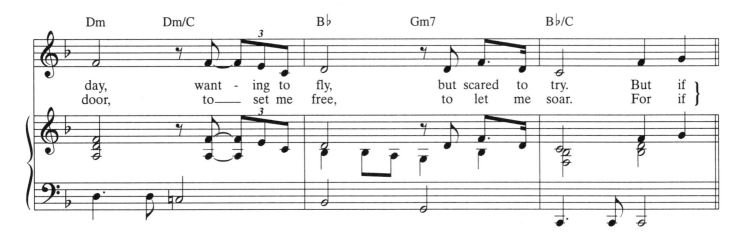

day, want - ing to fly, but scared to try. But if
door, to— set me free, to let me soar. For if

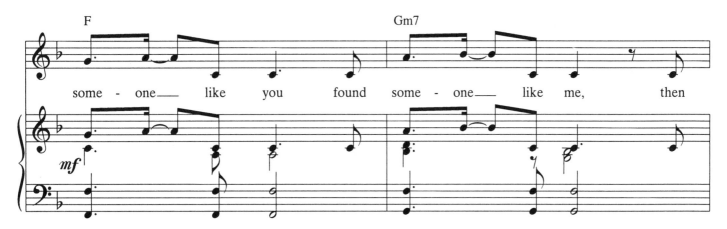

some - one— like you found some - one— like me, then

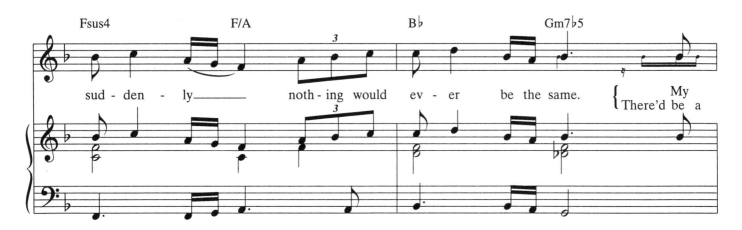

sud - den - ly— noth - ing would ev - er be the same. My
There'd be a

sud - den - ly_____ noth - ing would ev - er be the same. My

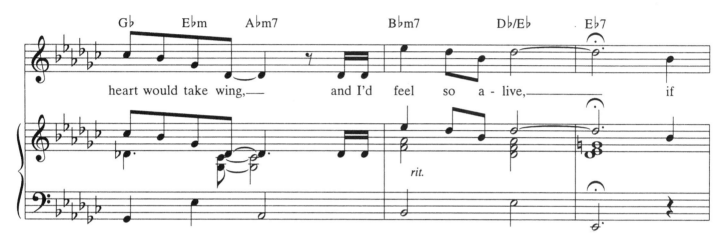

heart would take wing,____ and I'd feel so a - live,_____ if

Slower, freely

some - one like you loved me,_____ loved_

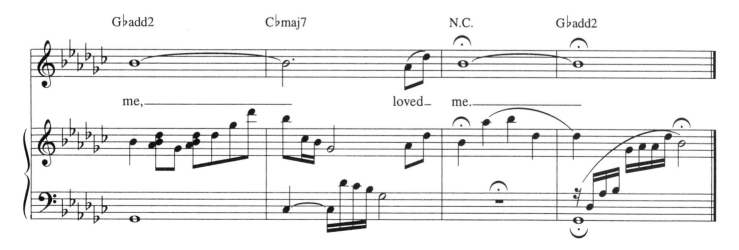

me,_____ loved_ me._____

A New Life

Words by Leslie Bricusse
Music by Frank Wildhorn

Moderately slow, freely

with pedal

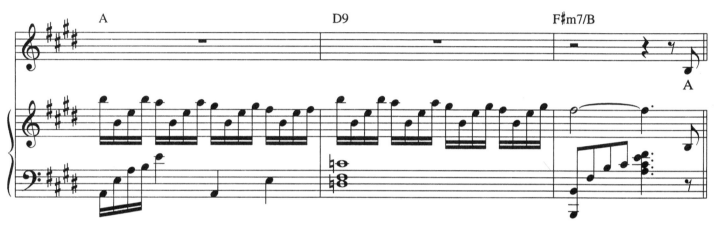

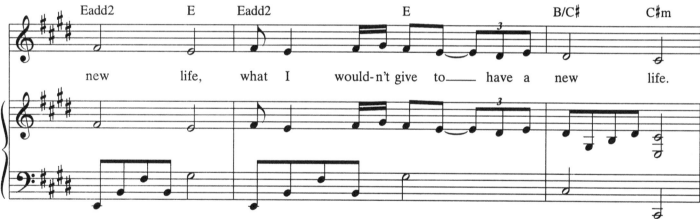

new life, what I would-n't give to___ have a new life.

One thing I have learned as I go through life,

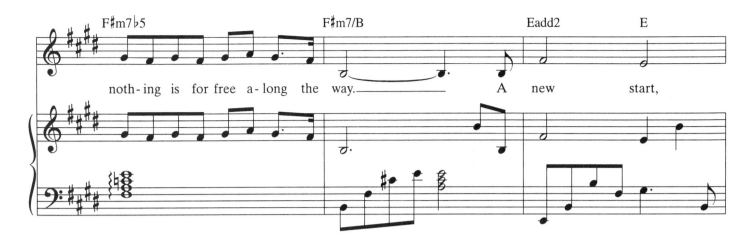

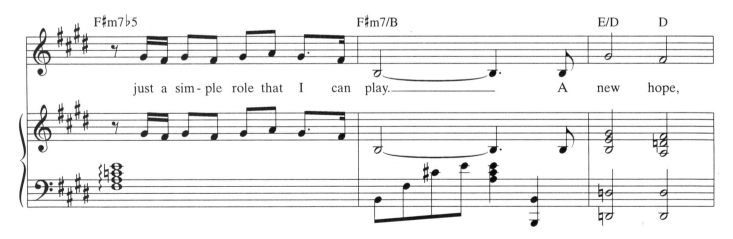

some-thing— to con-vince me— to re-new hope. A

new day, bright e-nough to help me find my way. A

new chance, one that may-be has a touch of ro-mance.

Where can it be,—— the chance for me? A

Moderately, in rhythm

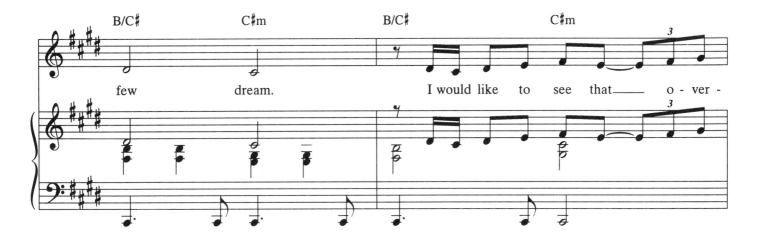

new dream,   I have one I know that___ ver - y

few dream.   I would like to see that___ o - ver -

due dream,   e - ven though it nev - er may come

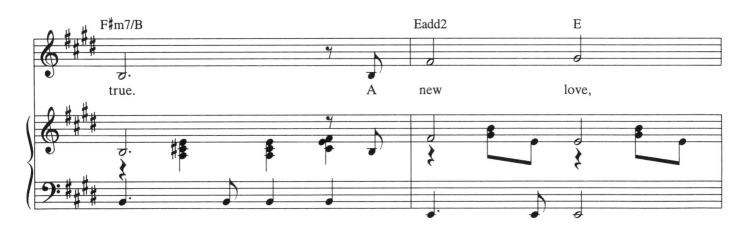

true.   A new love,

though I know there's no such___ thing as true love.

E - ven so, al - though I___ nev - er knew love,

still I feel that one dream___ is my due. A

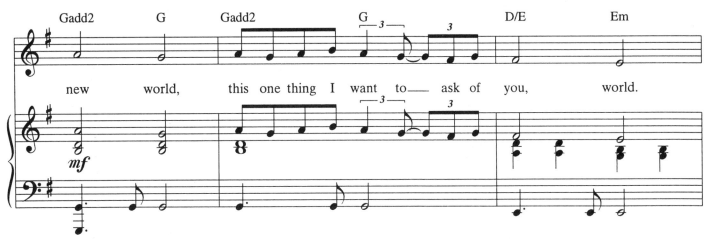

new world, this one thing I want to___ ask of you, world.

Once be - fore it's time___ to say a - dieu, world,

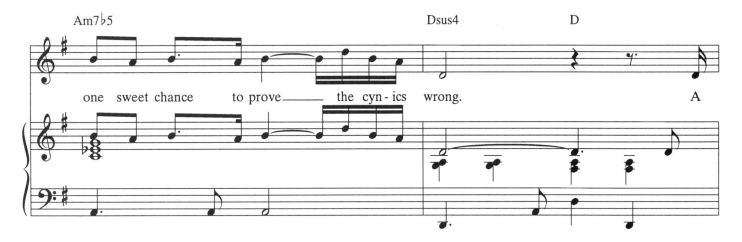

one sweet chance to prove___ the cyn - ics wrong. A

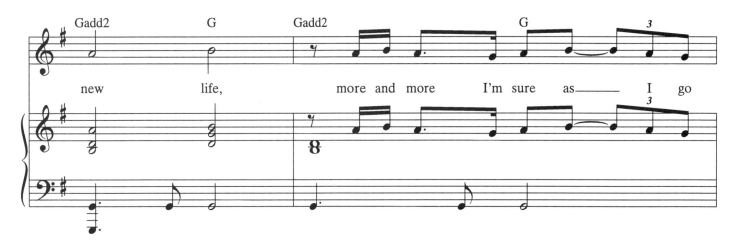

new life, more and more I'm sure as___ I go

through life. Just to play the game and to pur -

sue life, just to share its plea - sures and be -

long, that's what I've been here for all a -

long._____ Each day's a brand - new life._____

Curtain Calls!

New From Atlantic Theatre Recordings:

Jekyll & Hyde

Original Broadway Cast Album
Music by Frank Wildhorn
Lyrics by Leslie Bricusse

The Scarlet Pimpernel

Original Broadway Cast Album
Music by Frank Wildhorn
Lyrics by Nan Knighton

The star-studded concept recording of

The Civil War: An American Musical

by Frank Wildhorn, Jack Murphy and Gregory Boyd
Music by Frank Wildhorn

ATLANTIC THEATRE